Illustrator:
Jason M. Gadow

Editor:
Evan D. Forbes, M.S. Ed.

Editor-in-Chief:
Sharon Coan, M.S. Ed.

Art Director:
Elayne Roberts

Product Manager:
Phil Garcia

Imaging:
Rick Chacón

Cover Artist:
Keith Vasconcelles

Publishers:
Rachelle Cracchiolo, M.S. Ed.
Mary Dupuy Smith, M.S. Ed.

STUDIES
in a
BAG

PRIMARY

Author:
Deborah Shepard-Hayes

Teacher Created Materials, Inc.
P.O. Box 1040
Huntington Beach, CA 92647

Made in U.S.A.

ISBN-1-55734-198-2

Table of Contents

Table of Contents (cont.)

People from Different Times and Places Scavenger Hunts

Seasons, Symbols, and Holidays Scavenger Hunts

People at Work Scavenger Hunts

Maps, Graphs, and Directions Scavenger Hunts

Additional Forms

Introduction

Primary age students quickly move beyond their own personal areas to broaden their sense of place. It is now becoming increasingly important to provide this group of children with new insights about their communities and to help them make connections to the larger world of which they are a part. Providing a solid curricular base of literature, of math, of science, of real life lessons about real families, and of events in other times and places is essential.

What Is Social Studies in a Bag?

Welcome to the exciting and ever changing world of social studies in the classroom. In bygone years the teaching of social studies has often emphasized the memorizing of events and dates, activities not without value. Occasionally, however, this may have taken place with minimum regard for bringing to life different cultures and stories of the past or the need for all students to weave their own lives into the ongoing tapestry of human history. Present and relevant goals of the social studies curriculum emphasize the total development of students to become literate, fully functioning, interactive citizens. Through the social studies curriculum, individuals can gain knowledge, skills, and civic values which are necessary to become active and reflective participants in the world of the twenty-first century.

Using this book you will first find intriguing activities that involve the student's entire family. Second, you will find practical activities that reinforce lessons you are teaching in the classroom and promote real life application. Finally, you will find many follow-up classroom suggestions for activities to correlate with homework and extend its boundaries, challenge students, and bring social studies to life for your students.

How to Use This Book

Using a Pre-formatted Scavenger Hunt:

- Choose one of the pre-formatted scavenger hunts.
- Select a date the scavenger hunt is due and write it on the list for your students.
- Each scavenger hunt is set up in an easy, reproducible form. A copy should be made for each student.
- Staple the lists to large brown-paper grocery bags and give one to each student.
- Have students take the paper bags home and complete their assignment.
- When the paper bags have been returned, use the follow-up activities created especially for the scavenger hunt you chose.

Creating Your Own Scavenger Hunt:

- Create a theme or a topic to make your own personalized scavenger hunt.
- Select items that best fit the age, interests, and ability level of your students.
- List several items on a blank scavenger hunt list provided on page 77.
- Include a date due on your scavenger hunt list.
- Each scavenger hunt is set up in an easy, reproducible form. A copy should be made for each student.
- Staple the lists to large brown-paper grocery bags and give one to each student.
- Have students take the paper bags home and complete their assignment.
- When the paper bags have been returned, provide follow-up activities based on the items on your scavenger hunt list. The follow-up activities already in this book will provide some excellent suggestions for you to use.

Scavenger Hunt Suggestions

Providing social studies scavenger hunts for your class will be educational, exciting, and fun. Here are a few helpful suggestions before you begin.

- Have students take home the introductory letter found on page 7 to parents/guardians. This letter clearly explains how the social studies scavenger hunt will be conducted. The letter should answer any questions parents/guardians may have, as well as promote excitement for this new activity.
- Send home the supply request letter (page 8) asking for paper grocery bags. Parents/guardians should be eager to supply the bags needed for the scavenger hunts.
- Recycle the brown-paper grocery bags whenever possible. Encourage your students to care for and return their grocery bags after each scavenger hunt is complete.
- Allow approximately four to seven days for your students to complete their scavenger hunt. It is best if the time period includes a weekend. This will allow your students to involve their entire families.
- Spend time discussing with students how they located the items found on their scavenger hunt list before beginning the follow-up activities.
- Plan ahead so holiday-related scavenger hunts may be enjoyed during the appropriate week.
- Use the awards that have been provided to recognize students who show exceptional enthusiasm and dedication. Special awards have been included for students who locate all of their items, as well as students who find items that were especially difficult.

Letter Home

Date__________________

Dear Parent/Guardian,

This week, we will be holding our ___________ social studies scavenger hunt. It promises to be an exciting activity that will include your entire family.

On ____________________________, your child will receive a scavenger hunt list stapled to a paper lunch bag. This list will identify several social studies-related items that your child will be asked to locate. Most of the items on your child's list may be found around the house. Some items may be easier to find than others. You and other family members are encouraged to help your child with the scavenger hunt.

- This scavenger hunt will motivate your child to think about and discuss social studies outside the classroom.
- It will reinforce math skills learned in the classroom, as well as encourage problem solving.
- It will provide a practical application of social studies in real life.
- Finally, the scavenger hunt will provide an unusual homework activity the whole family is sure to enjoy.

This scavenger hunt will be due on _______________ . Before the scavenger bag is brought back to school, have your child check the box next to each item that was found and sign your child's scavenger hunt list in the space provided.

Once the scavenger hunt bags have been brought back to school, we will follow up with hands-on activities involving all items that were found. All items will be returned on the following day they are due.

Watch for more exciting scavenger hunts in the weeks to come. I am confident that you will enjoy these unusual, challenging activities as much as your child does.

Sincerely,

Supply Request Letter

Getting Around Town Scavenger Hunt

Date Due: ______________________

- ❑ 1. A city bus ticket or token (or subway ticket) and bus (or subway) schedule.
- ❑ 2. A road map of your city.
- ❑ 3. A brochure about a new car (or truck, van, sports utility vehicle).
- ❑ 4. One bicycle lock.
- ❑ 5. One car key (could be a trunk or trailer key) and knowledge of the particular country where that car was made.
- ❑ 6. A walking shoe. (Be sure to know the country where it was made.)

GOOD LUCK!

Student's Name: ______________________

Parent's Signature: ______________________

Getting Around Town Scavenger Hunt

Date Due: ______________________

- ❑ 1. A city bus ticket or token (or subway ticket) and bus (or subway) schedule.
- ❑ 2. A road map of your city.
- ❑ 3. A brochure about a new car (or truck, van, sports utility vehicle).
- ❑ 4. One bicycle lock.
- ❑ 5. One car key (could be a trunk or trailer key) and knowledge of the particular country where that car was made.
- ❑ 6. A walking shoe. (Be sure to know the country where it was made.)

GOOD LUCK!

Student's Name: ______________________

Parent's Signature: ______________________

Getting Around Town Scavenger Hunt (cont.)

Follow-up Activities

- Encourage a class discussion about public transportation in your town, bus or subway. Ask students to share their experiences with public transportation. Be sure to let them share how they acquired their bus tickets, especially if they did not ride the bus themselves. Have them brainstorm the environmental advantages of using public transportation. Then have them plan a day of errands using their bus or subway schedules.
- Working with partners or in small groups, have students locate the following places using their city road maps.
  a. the school
  b. their homes
  c. the grocery store they go to
  d. the park closest to their house
  e. the city courthouse (or town square)
  f. the city bus station
  g. (add your own)
- Students can use small sticky-notes with a symbol for each item as they locate them on their maps. If maps do not need to be returned, students can use highlighter pens to circle the locations.
- Create a large graph to display the automobile brochure information. List columns for car, truck, van, sports utility vehicle, etc. Make small shapes representing each of these so students will have a tangible symbol to affix to the graph. When students share their brochures, ask them what country the vehicle was made in, locate the country on a map, and then have them paste their respective symbols on the graph. Group students according to vehicle type. These small groups will share brochures and then design their own "Ultimate Transportation Vehicle" on paper.
- Have students compare and contrast bike locks. They should use size, type, and shape when doing their comparisons. Encourage a class discussion of the advantages and disadvantages of using a bicycle for transportation.
- Have students create country maps, outlining them with their car keys. Locate your "car key" country on a map. Then trace that country on a piece of construction paper. Inside your map write the name of the country in which your car is produced. Outline the country, using your car key as the pattern, then color in the key shape. Finally, research what other products are made there.
- Have students compare walking shoes. Discuss with your class how walking is the world's oldest and most reliable form of transportation, yesterday and today. Have them determine where their shoes were manufactured. They should write their names, shoe types, and countries of origin on sticky-notes and place them on a class map. When all students have done this, draw conclusions about the different places shoes are made.

On the Road Again Scavenger Hunt

Date Due: ____________________

❑ 1. A toy vehicle from home that would run on the road if it were life size.

❑ 2. An automobile rules and regulations booklet from the Department of Motor Vehicles. (Browse through the booklet with your parent/guardian.)

❑ 3. A small cardboard box or round cereal box.

❑ 4. A picture of a road sign (from the newspaper, magazine, brochure, poster, etc.).

❑ 5. A United States map showing freeways and interstates.

GOOD LUCK!

Student's Name: ____________________

Parent's Signature: ____________________

On the Road Again Scavenger Hunt

Date Due: ____________________

❑ 1. A toy vehicle from home that would run on the road if it were life size.

❑ 2. An automobile rules and regulations booklet from the Department of Motor Vehicles. (Browse through the booklet with your parent/guardian.)

❑ 3. A small cardboard box or round cereal box.

❑ 4. A picture of a road sign (from the newspaper, magazine, brochure, poster, etc.).

❑ 5. A United States map showing freeways and interstates.

GOOD LUCK!

Student's Name: ____________________

Parent's Signature: ____________________

On the Road Again Scavenger Hunt (cont.)

Follow-up Activities

- Ask students what streets and roads are used for and why we need cars, trucks, and buses. Tell students the word *vehicle* is another word for cars, trucks, and buses and is something that carries people or things and moves them from one place to another. Ask students how these vehicles help people and things travel. Ask students how they travel to school today. Talk about other kinds of travel (e.g., airplane, train, bike, skateboard, walking, etc.).
- Have students share the toy vehicles they brought. Tape student's names to their vehicles as they will be grouped together for sorting and graphing. Make a large graph displaying information about the vehicles. Sort the vehicles by type, number of wheels, color, and size.
- Talk about the importance of following rules of the road. Ask students why it is important to have rules for drivers. Discuss with them what driving the roads would be like if there were not any rules. Encourage students to share their experiences of getting DMV booklets. Point out the pages about speed limits, passing other vehicles, and parking. Ask students to share what they know about a driver's license.
- Allow time for each student to share his/her road-sign cutouts. Group and classify the signs. Talk about the different signs. Ask students why many of the signs are pictures rather than words. Students can draw their own traffic signs on paper and share them with the class.
- Using small cardboard boxes, students can make a highway and road system on a large piece of mural paper. Give students construction paper, glue, scissors, and markers to create tunnels, bridges, and buildings. Have them use blue construction paper to make rivers and lakes. Use some of the smaller traffic sign cutouts for signs on the classroom road by gluing them to a square or circle shape from an index card, tape to a small stick, and affix to the mural with a chunk of clay. The actual road can be made with black construction paper and chalk marks. Before students play on the roadway, discuss the rules of the road. Allow small groups of students to "drive" their vehicles along the roadway, being sure to follow the rules of the road. Those who do not follow the rules will have their drivers' licenses revoked, just as adult drivers do.
- Have students open up their national maps. Tell them that they will be taking pretend drives with their fingers as the vehicles. Ask them to put their fingers on their home city and tell them the highway or interstate number on which they should drive. Give them a destination and let them run their fingers across the maps to their destinations. Be sure to ask them in what direction they are traveling as they go. Vary the game by telling students to travel a certain direction until they get to the next town, then ask what that town is. Allow students to choose and call destinations as well.

Oneth by Land, Twoeth by Sea, and Air Makes Three Scavenger Hunt

Date Due: ____________________

- ❑ 1. One lunch-box size milk or juice carton.
- ❑ 2. One balloon (round shape preferred).
- ❑ 3. One craft stick.
- ❑ 4. A picture, cut from a newspaper, magazine, brochure, etc., of a way to travel by land.
- ❑ 5. A picture, cut from a newspaper, magazine, brochure, etc., of a way to travel by sea.
- ❑ 6. A picture, cut from a newspaper, magazine, brochure, etc., of a way to travel by air.

GOOD LUCK!

Student's Name: ____________________

Parent's Signature: ____________________

Oneth by Land, Twoeth by Sea, and Air Makes Three Scavenger Hunt

Date Due: ____________________

- ❑ 1. One lunch-box size milk or juice carton.
- ❑ 2. One balloon (round shape preferred).
- ❑ 3. One craft stick.
- ❑ 4. A picture, cut from a newspaper, magazine, brochure, etc., of a way to travel by land.
- ❑ 5. A picture, cut from a newspaper, magazine, brochure, etc., of a way to travel by sea.
- ❑ 6. A picture, cut from a newspaper, magazine, brochure, etc., of a way to travel by air.

GOOD LUCK!

Student's Name: ____________________

Parent's Signature: ____________________

Oneth by Land, Twoeth by Sea, and Air Makes Three Scavenger Hunt (cont.)

Follow-up Activities

- Write the word *transportation* on the board and discuss (or review) the meaning. Tell students that depending on where a person travels, the mode of transportation may be different. Also explain that people choose different modes of transportation purely for enjoyment and recreation.

- Create a large transportation table by dividing a large sheet of butcher paper into three columns and label them *land, air,* and *water.* Have students glue each of their three pictures in the respective columns. Compare the different pictures and types of transportation. Talk about ways to further group the pictures within each column (e.g., all the trucks make one group, cars, buses, etc.).

- Have students share their transportation experiences for each of the three areas. Divide sheets of construction paper into three columns and label each *land, air,* and *water.* Have students draw pictures of their experiences. Display these around a large class table of information.

- Show a picture of a hot air balloon, if accessible; if not, sketch one for your students. Ask if anyone has ever ridden in one. Tell students that in the early part of the century hot air balloons were very popular and often found at fairs and other celebrations. Today hot air balloon travel is mostly recreational. Tell students they will be creating their own hot air balloons. First, have students blow up their balloons and tie off the ends. Then have them open up a small juice or milk carton, decorate it, and use it as the balloon basket. Tape a craft stick horizontally to the tied part of the balloon to attach the balloon to your basket. Two people will be needed; one person holds the balloon/stick into the opening of the carton, and the other person tapes strands of string or yarn from the top of the balloon to the bottom of the basket. Students can write about an imaginary journey they take in their hot air balloon.

- Have students create their own inventions allowing people to travel by land, water, and air. They can draw pictures or build models. Have them give these inventions a name. Then they can write letters and send their ideas to a car company. (Most car companies will respond by sending free material.)

Planes, Trains, and Trucks Scavenger Hunt

Date Due: ____________________

- ❑ 1. One shoe box.
- ❑ 2. One lunch-size milk carton.
- ❑ 3. A food item that was not grown or produced in your town.
- ❑ 4. A magazine or newspaper picture of a train, plane, and truck.
- ❑ 5. An item (or handful of an item) that can fit in the palm of your hand.

GOOD LUCK!

Student's Name: ____________________

Parent's Signature: ____________________

Planes, Trains, and Trucks Scavenger Hunt

Date Due: ____________________

- ❑ 1. One shoe box.
- ❑ 2. One lunch-size milk carton.
- ❑ 3. A food item that was not grown or produced in your town.
- ❑ 4. A magazine or newspaper picture of a train, plane, and truck.
- ❑ 5. An item (or handful of an item) that can fit in the palm of your hand.

GOOD LUCK!

Student's Name: ____________________

Parent's Signature: ____________________

Planes, Trains and Trucks Scavenger Hunt (cont.)

Follow-up Activities

- Write the words *airplane, train,* and *truck* on the board. Draw a picture next to each word. Survey students to determine how many of them have ridden on these. Differentiate between big rig and sports utility trucks. Tell students these modes of transportation are also used to transport goods as well as people. Talk about the speed at which each vehicle travels. Look at a world map and consider travel situations where all three modes would be necessary to transport one product.
- Have students share their food items. Ask them to tell where each food item came from. Have students use a state, nation, and/or world map to help locate the food's country of origin. Ask your class to talk about how they think each item got to their country.
- Have students pretend they are store owners. Ask them to draw a picture of one of the products their store sells. Then have them choose another town, state, or country where their product will be sold. Have them draw a world map (amount of detail will depend upon age) and make an X on their three location choices. Have them glue pictures of a train, truck, or plane on the appropriate routes used for this transportation. When finished, encourage students to share their products and choices for transporting the goods. If there are any extra pictures, make a class collage.
- Ask students to share what they know about big rig trucks. Encourage details like number of wheels, where they were seen, what the trucks looked like, etc. Tell them that some trucks have a built-in sleeping compartment. Ask students why trucks might have a place for sleeping. After looking at pictures of trucks, have students make their own big rigs out of shoe boxes. Have each student include a small school photo to place in the driver's seat. On the side panels of the truck students should draw or write a company name on their truck and what kinds of goods are carried.
- Explain what a freight train is to your students. Talk about the kinds of freight on trains (e.g., livestock, cars, lumber, canned goods, etc.). Mention refrigerator cars, too. Discuss the importance and advantages of using trains to transport goods. Have each student make a boxcar from a milk carton. Use construction paper and felt pens to make the wheels. Cut open one side of the carton to make a freight door. Have students load their box-cars with the small items they brought. Assign students to make the engine and caboose. Connect the train together with yarn and tape.
- Play the "Freight Relays" on the playground. Divide your class into relay teams. Each team becomes the train, truck, or plane. They must carry freight (e.g., a ball, sponge, book, etc.) and move like that mode of transportation (i.e., an airplane relay would have students run with their arms out like wings).

Take a Vacation Scavenger Hunt

Date Due: ______________________

- ❑ 1. Clipping of airline fares from the newspaper (usually found in travel or business section).
- ❑ 2. A vacation brochure (free at most travel agencies) or an advertisement for a vacation package.
- ❑ 3. A postcard (new or used).
- ❑ 4. A picture of a cruise ship (from a newspaper, magazine, or travel brochure).
- ❑ 5. A receipt for fuel from the gas station.
- ❑ 6. A piece of charcoal in a plastic bag.

GOOD LUCK!

Student's Name: ______________________

Parent's Signature: ______________________

Take a Vacation Scavenger Hunt

Date Due: ______________________

- ❑ 1. Clipping of airline fares from the newspaper (usually found in travel or business section).
- ❑ 2. A vacation brochure (free at most travel agencies) or an advertisement for a vacation package.
- ❑ 3. A postcard (new or used).
- ❑ 4. A picture of a cruise ship (from a newspaper, magazine, or travel brochure).
- ❑ 5. A receipt for fuel from the gas station.
- ❑ 6. A piece of charcoal in a plastic bag.

GOOD LUCK!

Student's Name: ______________________

Parent's Signature: ______________________

Take a Vacation Scavenger Hunt (cont.)

Follow-up Activities

- Write the word *vacation* on the board. Tell students that a vacation is a time for a person or family to take a break from work and relax. Explain that sometimes people go on vacations to places which are far from their homes, while others travel a short distance. Talk about the different ways of travel that people use to get to a vacation place. Ask students to share some of their vacation stories.
- Have students brainstorm different types of transportation and write them on the board (e.g., bike, car, train, bus, airplane, etc.). Explain that these transportation modes were invented at different times in history and have had an effect on the choices people have made regarding their travel. Make a time line of these modes of transportation. Talk about different vacation scenarios by asking students questions like, "If you lived in Canada and wanted to vacation in Hawaii and the year was 1920, how could you get to your destination?"
- Allow students to share their post cards with the group. Encourage them to tell as much about the post card destination as possible. Locate the destination of the post card on the appropriate map. Then in a large circle pass the post cards around so that everyone can get a closer look. Provide students index cards. Have them make their own post cards from a place that they have been. They can address it and write a message to someone in class.
- Ask students to share their cruise ship pictures. If any students have been on cruises, encourage them to share their experiences. Explain that a cruise ship is not only a mode of transportation but also a vacation in and of itself, because of all the activities aboard the ship. Make a large world map and ask students to color in the oceans. Label the oceans and have students glue their cruise ships on oceans they choose.
- Make a number line and plug in the individual gas receipt totals on the line. Explain the principal of miles-per-gallon (mpg). Use a state map and plot a drive across the state. Tell students the number of miles and have them estimate how many gallons of fuel it would take to get there. Estimate how much money would be spent on fuel.
- Tell students about the evolution of the train from the use of coal to steam to electric power. Explain the importance of the train in the early days of the nation. Tell students that coal is mined from the earth. Have students make sketches of trains, using their coal pieces, keeping the plastic bags on their hands as they draw. Spray hair spray over the drawings to hold the charcoal in place.
- Let students share their vacation brochures or travel packages information. Let students choose which places they would like to go and have them tell what types of transportation would be needed to get there, use there, and get back home.

Follow the Rules Scavenger Hunt

Date Due: ____________________

- ❑ 1. A cut-out a picture from a magazine showing someone or a group of people following rules.
- ❑ 2. One small paper plate.
- ❑ 3. Ten cotton balls.
- ❑ 4. Copy of the posted rules from a community place (e.g., library, pool, park, etc.).
- ❑ 5. Copy of a rule symbol on an index card (e.g., stop sign, street lights, yield sign, walk sign, etc.).

GOOD LUCK!

Student's Name: ____________________

Parent's Signature: ____________________

Follow the Rules Scavenger Hunt

Date Due: ____________________

- ❑ 1. A cut-out a picture from a magazine showing someone or a group of people following rules.
- ❑ 2. One small paper plate.
- ❑ 3. Ten cotton balls.
- ❑ 4. Copy of the posted rules from a community place (e.g., library, pool, park, etc.).
- ❑ 5. Copy of a rule symbol on an index card (e.g., stop sign, street lights, yield sign, walk sign, etc.).

GOOD LUCK!

Student's Name: ____________________

Parent's Signature: ____________________

Follow the Rules Scavenger Hunt (cont.)

Follow-up Activities

- Ask students what a rule is. Have them share their experiences where rules have both been followed and broken. Ask them why rules are important. In small groups have students share their magazine pictures of people following rules. Have students share what rule(s) they think is being followed and whether they agree with that rule or not. Make a class book of all the magazine pictures with student writing samples about the rules.
- Read the poem "Mary Had a Little Lamb" by Sara Josepha Hale. Reread the verse about how it was against the rules to bring pets to school. Talk about why that was a rule for school and whether or not it was a good rule. Ask students to share how they thought Mary felt about the rule. Discuss with students how it is important to follow rules, even if we do not always like them. Have students make their own lambs from the paper plates and cotton. Have them draw a face in the center of the plate, glue the cotton balls around the edge of the plate, and then cut out and glue on ears of construction paper.
- On a large piece of poster paper, survey students, using tally marks for community places they visited to research rules. Show students how to make tally marks for keeping track of numbers and information. Talk about the rules students found. Divide students into groups representing these places. Have them act out the rules while the rest of your class tries to guess what the rules are.
- Have students share their index cards of symbols. Talk about each symbol and what it means. Play "Flash-a-Rule" by collecting all of the cards and gathering students in a semi-circle. Flash the cards one at a time and have students act out the symbols in a game-like fashion.
- Visit the cafeteria at school during non-eating hours. Ask one of the workers to share the cafeteria rules with students. Encourage students to ask questions and make suggestions. Go back to class and have students make posters showing people following the cafeteria rules. Hang the posters in the cafeteria for the rest of the school to see.

Grocery Store Scavenger Hunt

Date Due: ______________________

- ❑ 1. Two coupons for products found at a grocery store.
- ❑ 2. Newspaper advertisement page listing items on sale at the grocery store.
- ❑ 3. One paper grocery sack.
- ❑ 4. A receipt from a grocery store.
- ❑ 5. An empty food box or container with the label still attached (e.g., a box of crackers, peanut butter jar, milk carton, box of raisins, butter container, unopened canned goods, etc.).
- ❑ 6. A bar code label.

GOOD LUCK!

Student's Name: ______________________

Parent's Signature: ______________________

Grocery Store Scavenger Hunt

Date Due: ______________________

- ❑ 1. Two coupons for products found at a grocery store.
- ❑ 2. Newspaper advertisement page listing items on sale at the grocery store.
- ❑ 3. One paper grocery sack.
- ❑ 4. A receipt from a grocery store.
- ❑ 5. An empty food box or container with the label still attached (e.g., a box of crackers, peanut butter jar, milk carton, box of raisins, butter container, unopened canned goods, etc.).
- ❑ 6. A bar code label.

GOOD LUCK!

Student's Name: ______________________

Parent's Signature: ______________________

Grocery Store Scavenger Hunt (cont.)

Follow-up Activities

- Begin the grocery store activities by discussing with your students their experiences at a grocery store. Students will show the paper bags they brought to class. Write down the names of the different grocery stores represented on the bags and tally how many students' families shop at each store. Talk about the importance of grocery stores. Ask your students to consider what their families would do if there were no grocery stores. Mention the old-fashioned general stores and how they differed from today's grocery stores. (Collect the bags and use them to hold the other items students brought in for this scavenger hunt.)
- Review with your class some of the newspaper advertisement pages, listing items on sale at the grocery stores. Discuss how advertising benefits both the consumer and retailer. Give each small group of students a handful of newspaper ads and each group will work together to prepare a pretend grocery shopping list. Students decide upon ten items to buy. Have them cut out the pictures and prices and glue them to a piece of paper to create their list. When all the groups are finished, compare the different lists for items chosen, as well as the best deals.
- Have students share their bar code labels. Compare the lines and numbers on the different labels. Tell your students how technology has evolved from hand-written price tags to the electronically read bar code labels. Ask students to share their observations of grocery checkers using bar codes.
- The Mini Grocery Store. (For this activity both the bar code labels and empty food containers will be used.) Tell students they will be creating a "mini" grocery store. Divide the items equally among small groups of students. Students will determine a price for each item and then glue or tape the bar code label to the item. Use a fine-tip felt pen to write the price in cardinal numbers. Grocery store items should have simple prices such as $.50, $1, or $2. Discuss reasonable prices with your students. Meet again as a whole group and collect the items. Group the items according to their appropriate categories (e.g., dairy, snacks, canned fruit, canned vegetables, etc.). Using shelves in a book case, a table, or a counter, set up a mini grocery store with the priced items. Small groups of students should take turns shopping at the store, using play money. Limit students to three or four items each. Assign one student to be the cashier.
- Review the coupons for various grocery items. Talk about how coupons can be helpful for saving money. Use coupons to help create subtraction problem-solving challenges. If any of the coupons are for products at the ministore, let students use them when shopping.

Journey to the Past Scavenger Hunt

Date Due: ______________________

- ❑ 1. Photograph of one or more of your ancestors as a child.
- ❑ 2. Family heirloom (any object, large or small, that has been passed down at least one generation).
- ❑ 3. An interesting story about one of your ancestors, either written down or recorded onto a cassette by an adult.
- ❑ 4. The name of the country that your surname comes from, using cut-out letters from a magazine.
- ❑ 5. An item from one parent's school days (e.g., report card, school picture, school book, etc.).

GOOD LUCK!

Student's Name: ______________________

Parent's Signature: ______________________

Journey to the Past Scavenger Hunt

Date Due: ______________________

- ❑ 1. Photograph of one or more of your ancestors as a child.
- ❑ 2. Family heirloom (any object, large or small, that has been passed down at least one generation).
- ❑ 3. An interesting story about one of your ancestors, either written down or recorded onto a cassette by an adult.
- ❑ 4. The name of the country that your surname comes from, using cut-out letters from a magazine.
- ❑ 5. An item from one parent's school days (e.g., report card, school picture, school book, etc.).

GOOD LUCK!

Student's Name: ______________________

Parent's Signature: ______________________

Journey to the Past Scavenger Hunt (cont.)

Follow-up Activities

- Emphasize to your students that history is a story about real events that have already happened. Compare history to your students' favorite story books. As much as they enjoy hearing their favorite story books, the stories of our families can be even more enjoyable because they are real and about our relatives. Throughout the day, or over the period of a few days, read students' family stories aloud or play the cassettes. If applicable, relate what is happening in world history at the time of each particular story.
- Students share their surname creations and tell in what country the name/family originates. Use a large world map and help students locate the country. On a small sticky-note write the name and country down and have students affix the note to the map on its appropriate location. Create an interesting bulletin board display with the original magazine surname creations.
- Set up a "Family Museum" in your classroom. Place family heirlooms on a table or counter. Write down the name of each student and respective family member (e.g., grandmother, great aunt, great grandfather, etc.) by each item. Have students take a tour through the museum, keeping in mind that museum rules apply here too—no touching! Invite another class to take a tour through the museum.
- Allow students time to share the items from their parents' school days with the whole class. Ask them to share any comments from their parents about how their school experience differed from their children's. Talk about the different types of schools in the early part of the century (i.e., one room with several grades) compared to the classes of today. Using a Venn diagram, students will compare and contrast their items from the past to similar items of the present. Both words and drawings can be used in the Venn diagram. Students may work in small groups and enlist the ideas of their team members.
- In small groups invite students to share their family photographs and tell as much as they know about the people (person) in the picture. Ask students to pretend that they lived during the times of the pictures and tell what life might have been like. What do they think school would have been like? What kinds of games would they have played? What kinds of clothes would they have worn? What might their chores have been?

Meet My Family Scavenger Hunt

Date Due: ____________________

- ❑ 1. A picture from a magazine showing a family.
- ❑ 2. A small item from each member of your family, which represents them in some way. (The item must fit into the bag. Items will be returned at the end of the class activity.)
- ❑ 3. Any item in which your family's name appears.
- ❑ 4. A photograph of your family.
- ❑ 5. A picture from a newspaper or magazine showing an activity that your family enjoys doing together.
- ❑ 6. A list of family chores.

GOOD LUCK!

Student's Name: ____________________

Parent's Signature: ____________________

Meet My Family Scavenger Hunt

Date Due: ____________________

- ❑ 1. A picture from a magazine showing a family.
- ❑ 2. A small item from each member of your family, which represents them in some way. (The item must fit into the bag. Items will be returned at the end of the class activity.)
- ❑ 3. Any item in which your family's name appears.
- ❑ 4. A photograph of your family.
- ❑ 5. A picture from a newspaper or magazine showing an activity that your family enjoys doing together.
- ❑ 6. A list of family chores.

GOOD LUCK!

Student's Name: ____________________

Parent's Signature: ____________________

Meet My Family Scavenger Hunt (cont.)

Follow-up Activities

- Have students share their magazine pictures. As students share their pictures, have them tell some of the similarities and differences between their families and the ones in the pictures. Conduct a random poll in your class by asking students to stand if these conditions apply to them:
    a. Students who have a sister.
    b. Students who have a brother.
    c. Students who have both a brother and sister.
    d. Students who have no brothers or sisters.
    e. Students who have extended family members living with them.
- Have students introduce their families to the rest of the class by sharing their personal items. Have them form small groups, and in those groups students can share the names of their family members, the items they brought in, and why each item represents that particular family member.
- Have students share the items with family names on them. Have them identify how many of the names are similar, how many start or end with the same letter, which names are long, which names are short, etc. Display these items on a countertop or table. Have small student groups take turns observing the objects and then placing them in alphabetical order. After the order has been checked by an adult, mix up the objects and have the next group come up and do the same thing.
- Have students make a family mobile using colored markers, crayons, large and small paper plates, string, and the photographs they brought in. Set aside a place in your classroom to hang the family mobiles.
- Create a large graph on butcher paper. Make several columns to include things like games, movies, sports, vacations, etc. Have students share the pictures of their families' favorite activities. Place a sticky-note with the student's name on each picture and then after each student has shared it with the class, tape it to the graph. When the graph is complete, discuss the results.
- Discuss with your students the importance of teamwork, especially within the family unit. Recognize the value of sharing responsibilities at home. Ask students to think about one of the jobs they do at home. Then have them fold a white piece of construction paper into eight squares. In square one have them draw a picture of themselves doing a chore at home. Then in the remaining seven squares, write the days of the week and mark an "X" in each day as the chore is completed.

Post Office Scavenger Hunt

Date Due: ______________

- ❑ 1. An envelope which has been mailed and shows the postmark clearly.
- ❑ 2. One plain, unused letter-size envelope.
- ❑ 3. Your zip code and the zip code of a relative not living in your same town written on a piece of paper.
- ❑ 4. A shoe box.
- ❑ 5. One stamp (used or new) featuring a picture of a person.
- ❑ 6. One piece of stationery.

GOOD LUCK!

Student's Name: ____________________________

Parent's Signature: __________________________

Post Office Scavenger Hunt

Date Due: ______________

- ❑ 1. An envelope which has been mailed and shows the postmark clearly.
- ❑ 2. One plain, unused letter-size envelope.
- ❑ 3. Your zip code and the zip code of a relative not living in your same town written on a piece of paper.
- ❑ 4. A shoe box.
- ❑ 5. One stamp (used or new) featuring a picture of a person.
- ❑ 6. One piece of stationery.

GOOD LUCK!

Student's Name: ____________________________

Parent's Signature: __________________________

Post Office Scavenger Hunt (cont.)

Follow-up Activities

- Ask students to share how they think a letter gets from one person to another. Ask them to share their experiences at the post office. Encourage them to talk about what they think happens at the post office and what kinds of jobs people have who work there.
- Draw an envelope on the board and include a destination address and return address. Show students where to put the to and from addresses. Circle the zip code. Explain what a zip code is and why it is important. Create a chart on the board with the zip code information students bring in. Tally the number of zip codes from relatives that are the same. Find out the smallest and largest zip codes and where they come from. Establish a pattern of increasing zip code numbers from one coast to another (in the United States).
- Have students pass around their postmarked envelopes to compare size, type, and return addresses. Ask students to look closely at the postmarks. They should be able to find a date, time, and city. Explain why dates of letters and their postmarks are sometimes different. Make a time line using the dates on the postmarks. Make a list of all the cities found on the postmarks and locate them on a state map (or country/world map, if applicable).
- Have students share their stamps with pictures of people. Ask them to identify as many of the people as possible. Ask them why they think these people got their pictures on a stamp. Create a collage with all the stamps and display it. Have students make stamps featuring their pictures. Include a price for postage. Make a collage of student-made stamps and display it next to the official stamp collage.
- Ask students to share what their mailboxes look like and where they are located (e.g., stand alone or community, front door, curb, decorative, plain, etc.). Explain that each individual's mail is private and it is against the law to tamper with a mailbox, or to read another person's mail without permission. Tell students that they will be creating their own post office in the classroom. Have students use shoe boxes for their mail box. Label them with student name and stack them to form pigeonholes. Use these boxes for notes home, letters to each other, and returned work. Students take turns being the sorter and mail carrier.
- Compare the stationery examples. Ask students why people might use printed stationery instead of plain paper. Sort according to style (e.g., monogrammed, floral, geometric design, colors, etc.). Poll to determine what style is the most popular. Have students design their own stationery on blank writing paper and make matching envelopes from the plain envelopes. Have students write letters to their parents and hand deliver them to their mailboxes at home.

School Days Scavenger Hunt

Date Due: ____________

❑ 1. A straw, napkin, or eating utensil from a lunchroom worker.
Lunchroom Worker's Signature: ____________

❑ 2. A band-aid, gauze, or other non-medicated first-aid item from the nurse.
Nurse's Signature: ____________

❑ 3. A cleaning rag, nut and/or screw, small plastic trash bag, or other non-toxic cleaning or repair item from the custodian.
Custodian's Signature: ____________

❑ 4. An overdue notice, discarded title or subject card, library card no longer in use, or some other library related item from the librarian.
Librarian's Signature: ____________

❑ 5. A reward sticker, note, or blank behavior contract, from the principal.
Principal's Signature: ____________

❑ 6. A sticky-note, blank Rolodex or student registration card, blank attendance form, school letterhead and/or envelope, or some other secretarial-related item from the secretary.
Secretary's Signature: ____________

GOOD LUCK!

Student's Name: ____________

Parent's Signature: ____________

School Days Scavenger Hunt

Date Due: ____________

❑ 1. A straw, napkin, or eating utensil from a lunchroom worker.
Lunchroom Worker's Signature: ____________

❑ 2. A band-aid, gauze, or other non-medicated first-aid item from the nurse.
Nurse's Signature: ____________

❑ 3. A cleaning rag, nut and/or screw, small plastic trash bag, or other non-toxic cleaning or repair item from the custodian.
Custodian's Signature: ____________

❑ 4. An overdue notice, discarded title or subject card, library card no longer in use, or some other library related item from the librarian.
Librarian's Signature: ____________

❑ 5. A reward sticker, note, or blank behavior contract, from the principal.
Principal's Signature: ____________

❑ 6. A sticky-note, blank Rolodex or student registration card, blank attendance form, school letterhead and/or envelope, or some other secretarial-related item from the secretary.
Secretary's Signature: ____________

GOOD LUCK!

Student's Name: ____________

Parent's Signature: ____________

School Days Scavenger Hunt (cont.)

Follow-up Activities

- This scavenger hunt requires considerations different from those for the other scavenger hunts in this book. For the "School Days" scavenger hunt, students will complete the hunt at school during the school day. Students will be organized into hunting groups with one student in charge of the bag. Inform school individuals who will be "hunted" ahead of time in order to choose times which best fit their schedules. Make arrangements so there will be enough items for each group and rotate the groups so they do not all end up in one place at the same time.

- Upon return from the scavenger hunt, have student groups empty their bags onto their group tables and review the contents. Monitor the groups to check whether students remember what item came from what staff members.

- As a large group, talk about the importance of each of these jobs in order to help keep the school running smoothly. Encourage students to discuss the jobs they found most interesting, most challenging, and most fun. Talk about how all of these people work to help students and why team work is important.

- In partners, ask each student to tell about what school worker's job they would most like to have and why.

- Using a large piece of chart paper, work with students to create a school map. Draw large shapes representing each of the buildings of your school. As you draw in the hallways and various buildings, ask students to identify where the respective rooms of the school workers are. Use a different color or symbol to represent each different area. Ask students how this map could be valuable to someone else. Post the map on a board so students can view it later. This will promote their understanding that maps help us find how to get to places.

- Using the items collected, each small group will create a collage using construction paper, tape, and/or glue. Ask groups to make titles for their collages, relating them to the topic of school workers. Write the title somewhere on the collage when it is complete.

- Divide students into six small groups and assign one of the school workers to each group. Each group will be responsible for drawing a thank-you card to that person. Be sure to invite these individuals to visit your class and look at the collages.

Across the Land Scavenger Hunt

Date Due: ______________________

- ❑ 1. One piece of aluminum foil about 12" x 12" (30 cm x 30 cm).
- ❑ 2. One piece of plastic cling wrap about 12" x 12" (30 cm x 30 cm).
- ❑ 3. Five small rocks.
- ❑ 4. One handful of grass and/or weeds, in a plastic bag.
- ❑ 5. One handful of sand, in a plastic bag.
- ❑ 6. A few small twigs or one twig about a foot (30 cm) long broken into smaller pieces.

GOOD LUCK!

Student's Name: ______________________

Across the Land Scavenger Hunt

Date Due: ______________________

- ❑ 1. One piece of aluminum foil about 12" x 12" (30 cm x 30 cm).
- ❑ 2. One piece of plastic cling wrap about 12" x 12" (30 cm x 30 cm).
- ❑ 3. Five small rocks.
- ❑ 4. One handful of grass and/or weeds, in a plastic bag.
- ❑ 5. One handful of sand, in a plastic bag.
- ❑ 6. A few small twigs or one twig about a foot (30 cm) long broken into smaller pieces.

GOOD LUCK!

Student's Name: ______________________

Across the Land Scavenger Hunt (cont.)

Follow-up Activities

- Ask students to look out the window and describe the land they see. Then ask them to tell about the kind of land around their homes in the town in which they live. Write the descriptive features on the board as students share. Tell students that if they lived in a different town, state, or country the land may be very different from where they are today.
- Show students a map of the country which highlights physical features. Refer to the map key for symbols representing the different features. Ask students to suggest some other symbols which could also represent these features. Point out the different land features (e.g., mountains, grasslands, deserts, lakes, etc.). Establish the connection between a group of states in one region having similar terrain. If any of your students have traveled to other regions, encourage them to share what the land looked like.
- Point out the major geographical features of your country. In the USA show the Appalachian Mountain Range, the Grand Canyon, the Great Lakes, the Mississippi River, Mt. McKinley, and the Rocky Mountains. In Mexico show the Gulf of California, the Isthmus of Tehuantepec, Oriental Mountain Ranges, and Sierra Madre Occidental. In Canada show the Hudson Bay, Mackenzie River, the Rocky Mountains, and the many bays and islands that exist in the country.
- Have students use their scavenger hunt materials to build a model map of their country. On a piece of tagboard or cardboard, draw the outline of your country. Pencil in the various geographical and physical features. Use rocks for any mountains, glue grass on for grasslands and prairies, use aluminum foil for rivers and cling wrap for lakes and bays, sprinkle sand for beaches, and glue the small twigs for large forest areas. When students share their map models, have them identify each geographical feature on their maps.
- Once the map models have been evaluated and shared, allow students to add to and modify their maps in order to create their own pretend countries. They may want to bring other items from home, or more of the same, to add to their maps. When they are complete, have them design a treasure hunt using directional words (N, S, E, W) on their maps. An X can be written in black pen and then camouflaged by the land features to indicate where the treasure is.

Corny Corn Scavenger Hunt

Date Due: ____________________

- ❑ 1. A food product that is made from corn.
- ❑ 2. A coupon for a corn product in the grocery store.
- ❑ 3. One plastic bag of unpopped corn kernels.
- ❑ 4. A commercial, magazine, or newspaper picture of any corn product.
- ❑ 5. A corny joke.
- ❑ 6. Four words cut out from a newspaper or magazine that rhyme with corn.

GOOD LUCK!

Student's Name: ____________________

Parent's Signature: ____________________

Corny Corn Scavenger Hunt

Date Due: ____________________

- ❑ 1. A food product that is made from corn.
- ❑ 2. A coupon for a corn product in the grocery store.
- ❑ 3. One plastic bag of unpopped corn kernels.
- ❑ 4. A commercial, magazine, or newspaper picture of any corn product.
- ❑ 5. A corny joke.
- ❑ 6. Four words cut out from a newspaper or magazine that rhyme with corn.

GOOD LUCK!

Student's Name: ____________________

Parent's Signature: ____________________

Corny Corn Scavenger Hunt (cont.)

Follow-up Activities

- Have students compare the many different food products that have been brought to class. Have students classify their products according to the meals at which they would be eaten. Discuss with your class which products have the most nutritional value, the least. Create a corn graph, using *Breakfast, Lunch, Dinner,* and *Snack* as the headings. Then have students tape each food product in the appropriate column and tally the results.

- Collect, read, and compare the different coupons for corn products. Have your class compare coupons of the greatest and least values. Discuss with students the value of using coupons when grocery shopping and the importance of budgeting money.

- Give each student one kernel of unpopped corn. Provide a graphic overview or flow chart illustrating the commercial cycle of corn (i.e., farm-factory-store-home). Discuss with students how each individual kernel of corn is, in fact, a seed. When the kernel is planted, it will grow into a plant that will produce corn. Have students share their experiences of eating corn. Pop some corn for your class to share.

- Ask students to share their pictures of corn. Have them tell what part of the corn cycle their pictures represent. Share with students how over the centuries corn has played an important role in many different cultures around the world. Create a classroom corn collage by drawing and coloring a large ear of corn in the middle of a large piece of construction paper and have students glue or tape their corn pictures to the poster.

- Produce a "Corny Comedy Show" in your classroom. Invite other classes to come and hear your students tell their corny jokes. Create a class book where corny jokes can be recorded for all corny joke lovers.

- Ask students to share their four rhyming corn words. As the words are being shared, create a master classroom list of all the words that rhyme with corn. Have students count all the words that have been used more than once. Finally, have them write poems using some of the words from the class list.

Down on the Farm Scavenger Hunt

Date Due: ____________________

- ❑ 1. One label from a can of food.
- ❑ 2. One label from a food product made from wheat (e.g., bread, crackers, pasta, etc.).
- ❑ 3. One egg carton.
- ❑ 4. One package of vegetable seeds (e.g., tomato, cucumber, broccoli, carrots, etc.).
- ❑ 5. One plastic or durable paper cylinder container which is sturdy enough to be punctured but not broken (i.e., potato chip container, frozen juice concentrate container, raisins container, etc.).

GOOD LUCK!

Student's Name: ____________________

Parent's Signature: ____________________

Down on the Farm Scavenger Hunt

Date Due: ____________________

- ❑ 1. One label from a can of food.
- ❑ 2. One label from a food product made from wheat (e.g., bread, crackers, pasta, etc.).
- ❑ 3. One egg carton.
- ❑ 4. One package of vegetable seeds (e.g., tomato, cucumber, broccoli, carrots, etc.).
- ❑ 5. One plastic or durable paper cylinder container which is sturdy enough to be punctured but not broken (i.e., potato chip container, frozen juice concentrate container, raisins container, etc.).

GOOD LUCK!

Student's Name: ____________________

Parent's Signature: ____________________

Down on the Farm Scavenger Hunt (cont.)

Follow-up Activities

- Ask your students to talk about the importance of food. Ask them to brainstorm the many places where food comes from. Lead the conversation in the direction of farming. Ask students to share any experience they have had with farming activities (e.g., living on or visiting a farm, planting a garden, seeing pictures of a farm, etc.). Tell students that there are many different types and sizes of farms. Write these words on the board: dairy, orchard, fishery, rice paddy, chicken ranch, and plantation. Talk about the different crops and livestock that are grown and raised at these places.
- Have students share their canned goods labels. Sort and categorize the different types of foods represented. Create a large bar graph showing the different food types. Ask students to glue their labels on the appropriate column of the graph. Discuss and draw conclusions from the information.
- Have students share their wheat product labels. Ask them if they have ever seen wheat while it is still growing in the soil. If you have a picture of wheat, show it; if not, draw a sketch on the board. Tell students that once the wheat grass is harvested, it is crushed and ground into flour. From this flour many products can be made (refer to the products students brought in). On a map show students where the major wheat producing states are (Great Plains, California, and Washington). Tally the number of similar wheat product labels.
- Ask students what things they think are needed in order for crops to grow. Lead them to understand that water, sunshine, and fertile soil are important factors. Ask them how they think a farmer waters his or her crops? Write their ideas on the board and then write the word irrigation. Tell students that irrigation means bringing water to dry land. Explain different irrigation techniques such as ditches and piped-in water. Create examples of irrigation by poking holes in the cylinder containers the students brought in. Students can make miniature ditches in the sandbox. Tell them that their ditches should be spaced the same distance the holes in their cylinders are. Lay the cylinders across the top line of the ditches. Use a garden watering can and pour water into the cylinders so students can observe the distribution of water.
- Set up miniature farms in the classroom, using seed and egg cartons. You will need potting soil for this activity. Students can plant one entire farm with just one seed type or share seeds with friends and plant two or three crops. Have students make little signs with index cards and toothpicks, naming the crops and farm. Talk about ways to care for the farms. When the seedlings are large enough, send the plants home for students to transplant or keep some and watch them grow all year.

Sea to Shining Sea Scavenger Hunt

Date Due: ____________________

- ❑ 1. A picture of something that lives in the ocean (plant or animal).
- ❑ 2. A handful of sand in a plastic bag.
- ❑ 3. Three words cut from a newspaper or magazine which have to do with the ocean (e.g., wave, surf, whale, ship, sea, blue, Pacific, etc.).
- ❑ 4. A handful of salt in a plastic bag.
- ❑ 5. One small rock.

GOOD LUCK!

Student's Name: ____________________

Parent's Signature: ____________________

Sea to Shining Sea Scavenger Hunt

Date Due: ____________________

- ❑ 1. A picture of something that lives in the ocean (plant or animal).
- ❑ 2. A handful of sand in a plastic bag.
- ❑ 3. Three words cut from a newspaper or magazine which have to do with the ocean (e.g., wave, surf, whale, ship, sea, blue, Pacific, etc.).
- ❑ 4. A handful of salt in a plastic bag.
- ❑ 5. One small rock.

GOOD LUCK!

Student's Name: ____________________

Parent's Signature: ____________________

Sea to Shining Sea Scavenger Hunt (cont.)

Follow-up Activities

- Show students a globe. Ask them to determine if there is more land or water. Do the same for a world map. Tell students that more than half of the earth's surface is covered with water. Explain that these large bodies of water are called oceans. Point out the four oceans by name. Have students share what they know about oceans and any visits they may have taken there.

- Have students share their pictures of ocean-related items. Make a large chart sorting the information. Possibilities for organization could be animal, plant, color, size, texture, etc.

- Write the words *coast* and *erosion* on the board. Tell students that a coast is the land along the edge of an ocean. Explain that after a long time of waves crashing against the coast, the soil and rocks begin to wear down and get carried away. This process is called erosion. Have students carefully look at some grains of sand. Point out the different colors. Ask them where they think sand comes from and how it is made. Explain that the constant pounding of waves onto rocks and shells eventually breaks them down into small pieces. This takes many years and eventually creates sand.

- On a map of the United States, locate the Mississippi River. (You may also want to locate other large rivers.) Ask students to list the similarities and differences between rivers and oceans. Point out the one similarity is the effect of erosion (like the Grand Canyon) and one difference is that the ocean is made of salty water. Tell students that most fresh water animals (except salmon) cannot live in the ocean because of the salt, and vice versa.

- Have students make a diagram illustrating the effects of ocean erosion. On a piece of tagboard, have students write the word "ocean" in glue, then sprinkle salt over the letters. Next they will write a + sign and glue the rock down. Write the = sign and then spread some glue down to sprinkle the sand upon.

- Ask students to share their three ocean-related words. Put the words into a container and mix them up. Students will work with partners and draw five words from the container. The partners will write a poem about the oceans, using each of these words at least once.

Trash Busters Scavenger Hunt

Date Due: ____________________

- ❑ 1. A used aluminum product.
- ❑ 2. A used paper product.
- ❑ 3. A used glass product.
- ❑ 4. An item which has the words "Printed on Recycled Paper" appearing on it.
- ❑ 5. An item which has a recycle symbol printed on it.
- ❑ 6. Call your local recycling center and ask for their operating hours and days. Write this information on a sheet of paper.

GOOD LUCK!

Student's Name: ____________________

Parent's Signature: ____________________

Trash Busters Scavenger Hunt

Date Due: ____________________

- ❑ 1. A used aluminum product.
- ❑ 2. A used paper product.
- ❑ 3. A used glass product.
- ❑ 4. An item which has the words "Printed on Recycled Paper" appearing on it.
- ❑ 5. An item which has a recycle symbol printed on it.
- ❑ 6. Call your local recycling center and ask for their operating hours and days. Write this information on a sheet of paper.

GOOD LUCK!

Student's Name: ____________________

Parent's Signature: ____________________

Trash Busters Scavenger Hunt (cont.)

Follow-up Activities

- Collect environmental and recycling information to share with students. Use your new information to compare the recycling of trash in your community/country to other communities/countries. Discuss with students the importance of conserving our natural resources for reasons of beauty and for use by future generations. Visit your local recycling center or have a representative speak to your class and provide further information about recycling.
- Label four boxes Aluminum, Glass, Paper, and Plastic and keep them in your classroom. Then have students share with the class their four items and deposit them in the proper box. Discuss with students the recycling process of these four products and how they are used to create other useful products.
- Using tape, glue, pins, and the products students brought to class, have them work in small groups to create a "Trash Busters" collage. After their "Trash Busters" collages have been created, display them in class. Then have students write stories about "The Adventures of Trash Buster" to share with the class.
- Have students share their "Printed on Recycled Paper" products. Review with students how new products are made into recycled products. Have students share and then collect their recycle symbols. Group the symbols by size, shape, color, texture, etc. Then have students use the symbols to make posters promoting recycling. Have them create their own environmental symbols for things like biodegradable, conservation, Earth Day, Protect the Environment, etc.
- Have students collect trash for one week at school and deposit what can be recycled in the classroom recycle boxes. Have students share any new feelings they have about taking care of their environment. At the end of the week, take the recycled materials to a community recycling center. Any money collected may be placed in a class party fund or used for an environmental project at school.

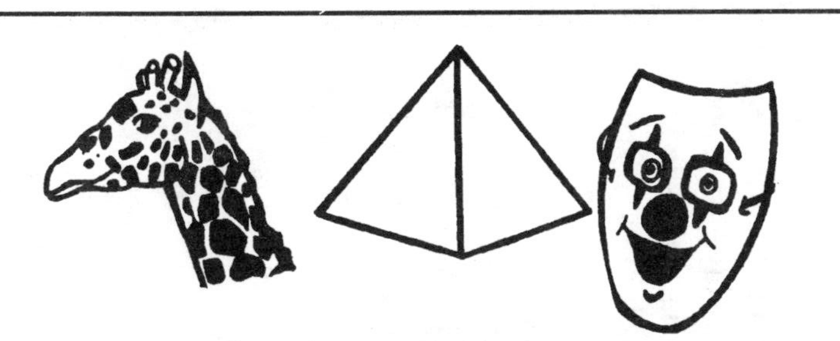

Passport to Africa Scavenger Hunt

Date Due: ____________________

- ❏ 1. A picture of an animal found in Africa (e.g., baboon, jackal, zebra, water buffalo, leopard, rhinoceros, antelope, wart hog, python, flamingo, giraffe, hippopotamus, elephant, etc.).
- ❏ 2. A piece of cotton fabric (e.g., t-shirt, rag, towel, etc.).
- ❏ 3. A mask (e.g., Halloween, costume party, or simple eye mask).
- ❏ 4. Something in the shape of a pyramid.
- ❏ 5. A small bag of corn meal.
- ❏ 6. Wear clothing with many different colors to school __________.

GOOD LUCK!

Student's Name: ____________________

Parent's Signature: ____________________

Passport to Africa Scavenger Hunt

Date Due: ____________________

- ❏ 1. A picture of an animal found in Africa (e.g., baboon, jackal, zebra, water buffalo, leopard, rhinoceros, antelope, wart hog, python, flamingo, giraffe, hippopotamus, elephant, etc.).
- ❏ 2. A piece of cotton fabric (e.g., t-shirt, rag, towel, etc.).
- ❏ 3. A mask (e.g., Halloween, costume party, or simple eye mask).
- ❏ 4. Something in the shape of a pyramid.
- ❏ 5. A small bag of corn meal.
- ❏ 6. Wear clothing with many different colors to school __________.

GOOD LUCK!

Student's Name: ____________________

Parent's Signature: ____________________

Passport to Africa Scavenger Hunt (cont.)

Follow-up Activities

- Show your students on a world map where Africa is located. Ask them to tell you in what direction Africa is from your country. Tell them that Africa is a continent made up of several countries. Make a list on chart paper titled "What We Know About Africa" and "What We Would Like to Know About Africa." Brainstorm with students to complete the chart.
- Tell students that Africa is home to many interesting and exotic animals. Have them share their pictures of African animals. Write the word *safari* on the board. Explain that a safari is a trip to look at the many different animals. At one time hunters went on safaris to kill animals, but today most safaris are for taking photographs and enjoying animals. Have students make a large mural by drawing trees, grass, rivers, and hills. Have them glue their animals onto the mural. Next draw a picture of a large school bus with enough windows for the number of students in your class. Have students draw their pictures in the windows. Title the mural, "Our Class Safari Trip to Africa" and display it.
- On the day your students wear their multi-colored clothing, make tie-dye coffee filters. If you have any pictures of African citizens wearing traditional tie-dyed clothes, share them with students. Tell students that Africans, both past and present, like to wear clothing with brilliant colors and bold patterns. On the western coast of the continent people are known for the special way they color fabric, known as tie-dyeing. Ask students to share any experiences they have had with tie-dyeing. Have students bunch up their pieces of fabric and, using string, tie the bunches in place. Then set up small pie tins of colored dye. Have students dip their fabrics in different colors and make a design. When they have finished dipping their fabrics, have them cut off the strings and unravel their fabrics to see their tie-dye designs.
- Tell students that people of African tribes make masks to celebrate different occasions. People of important positions in the tribe wear unique masks, too. Organize a parade with your students wearing their masks. March in class or visit another class. Have them write short descriptions (or draw pictures), telling what the significance of their masks would be if they were members of an African tribe.
- Draw a pyramid on the board. If you have pictures of Egyptian pyramids, share these with students. Locate Egypt on the map. Tell students that African people of earlier times built these great pyramids. Ask students to brainstorm how they think the pyramids could have been built without the aid of modern construction equipment. Have them share their pyramid shapes.
- Find the country of Kenya on the map of Africa. Tell students that in the area around the city of Nairobi the soil is rich and many crops are grown and exported, one of which is corn. Make corn porridge (mush) from the corn meal brought in. Tell students the African tribes of the past often ate corn porridge.

Passport to Canada Scavenger Hunt

Date Due: ____________________

- ❏ 1. One rubber or plastic glove.
- ❏ 2. Two plastic, styrofoam, or paper containers of different sizes and shapes (e.g., butter tub, popsicle mold, film canister, juice container, paper cups, balloon, bowls, etc.).
- ❏ 3. A cowboy hat. (This will be returned!)
- ❏ 4. One bar of Ivory® soap.
- ❏ 5. The words *French* and *English* cut out of a newspaper or magazine.

GOOD LUCK!

Student's Name: ____________________

Parent's Signature: ____________________

Passport to Canada Scavenger Hunt

Date Due: ____________________

- ❏ 1. One rubber or plastic glove.
- ❏ 2. Two plastic, styrofoam, or paper containers of different sizes and shapes (e.g., butter tub, popsicle mold, film canister, juice container, paper cups, balloon, bowls, etc.).
- ❏ 3. A cowboy hat. (This will be returned!)
- ❏ 4. One bar of Ivory® soap.
- ❏ 5. The words *French* and *English* cut out of a newspaper or magazine.

GOOD LUCK!

Student's Name: ____________________

Parent's Signature: ____________________

Passport to Canada Scavenger Hunt (cont.)

Follow-up Activities

- Show your students on a world map, where Canada is located. If applicable, ask them to tell you in what direction Canada is from their country. Make a list on chart paper titled "What We Know About Canada" and "What We Would Like to Know About Canada." Brainstorm with students to complete the chart. Ask students what kind of weather is common in Canada. Tell them it gets very cold in Canada and snows often.
- Tell students in Canada two languages are spoken, French and English. Show students on a world map where France is located. Ask students why they think Canadians speak French. Tell them the majority of early European settlers in Canada were French and that the French influence is strong even today. Draw a line down the middle of a piece of construction paper. Have students glue their *French* words to one side and the *English* words to the other. Ask them to talk about the advantages of knowing two different languages and brainstorm what challenges a country faces by having more than one language.
- Locate Quebec City on a map of Canada. Tell students this is the oldest city in Canada and still is mostly French speaking. Also tell them the most famous Canadian carnival is held there—the Winter Carnival. One popular activity at the carnival is ice sculpting. Have students create their own ice sculptures using the containers. Mix pitchers of water with different colors of food coloring. Have students fill their containers with two different colors, being sure to leave a little room at the top of the container for expansion. Using rubber bands tie loose containers such as plastic bags and rubber gloves. Place in a freezer overnight (unless you live in a very cold environment and can just place them outside). When the shapes are completely frozen, remove them from their containers by running a little warm water over them. You may need to cut some of the containers—the plastic cups, bags, and gloves. In small groups stack the pieces any way you like on a cookie tray. Invite another class in to view your Winter Wonderland. (But hurry, these sculptures will change their forms quickly.)
- Ask students if they have heard of a rodeo. Tell them rodeos are contests in which people demonstrate how well they can ride horses or do other ranch chores. The Canadian town of Calgary hosts the Calgary Stampede each year, the biggest rodeo in the world. Have your students wear their cowboy hats and host your own rodeo on the playground by having races and other contests.
- Tell students the first people living in Canada were the Inuits (also known as Eskimos). An Inuit traditional art form is ivory and soapstone carving. Students can carve their own animals from soap bars, using dull scissors and craft sticks.

Passport to Japan Scavenger Hunt

Date Due: ______________________

- ❑ 1. One set of chopsticks.
- ❑ 2. One tea bag.
- ❑ 3. One plastic bag full of white rice.
- ❑ 4. A picture of a fish, cut from a magazine, newspaper, computer, etc..
- ❑ 5. An advertisement for a Japanese-made automobile (e.g., Nissan, Honda, Mitsubishi, etc.).
- ❑ 6. Any product that was made in Japan.
- ❑ 7. Two plastic or styrofoam cups.

GOOD LUCK!

Student's Name: ______________________

Parent's Signature: ______________________

Passport to Japan Scavenger Hunt

Date Due: ______________________

- ❑ 1. One set of chopsticks.
- ❑ 2. One tea bag.
- ❑ 3. One plastic bag full of white rice.
- ❑ 4. A picture of a fish, cut from a magazine, newspaper, computer, etc..
- ❑ 5. An advertisement for a Japanese-made automobile (e.g., Nissan, Honda, Mitsubishi, etc.).
- ❑ 6. Any product that was made in Japan.
- ❑ 7. Two plastic or styrofoam cups.

GOOD LUCK!

Student's Name: ______________________

Parent's Signature: ______________________

Passport to Japan Scavenger Hunt (cont.)

Follow-up Activities

- Show your students on a world map, where Japan is located. Tell them the country is made up of four large islands and about 3,000 smaller ones. Make a list on chart paper titled "What We know About Japan" and "What We Would Like to Know About Japan." Brainstorm with students to complete the chart.
- Tell students that rice is a very important food in Japan. Rice is eaten at virtually every meal, and is also a primary export of Japan. Using some of the rice students collected, prepare enough cooked rice so that your entire class can taste some. Have students use their chopsticks to eat their rice. Encourage students to talk about the experience of using chopsticks as compared to forks and spoons. (Be sure students wash and save their chopsticks.)
- Tea is the traditional and most popular beverage in Japan. It is served at every meal, as well as at special ceremonies. Ask students to share what kind of tea bag they brought (e.g., herbal, flavored, Japanese, Chinese, etc.). Use large graph paper and make a graph showing the numbers of the different kinds of teas brought in by students. Have warm water available for your class and using students' tea bags and cups, make some tea for all the students.
- Ask students to share the names of Japanese-made cars. Have them glue their car names on index cards. Create a bar graph of different names and have students place their cards in the appropriate places on the graph. Point out the distance between Japan and North America. Ask students how they think cars made in Japan get to North America.
- Tell students that the rice industry is a very important business to Japan. Point to the map of Japan again and ask them why they think more fishing is done there than in other countries. Much of Japanese art is about nature, and a traditional type of painting is done with a real fish. Have students glue their fish pictures onto small rectangular pieces of construction paper. Using crayons, markers, or colored pencils, decorate the paper. Then tape chopsticks to both ends of the paper and create a scroll. Hang the scrolls around your class.
- Allow students time to share their Japanese-made products. Compare how many of the products are the same. Ask students if their products are made only in Japan or whether other countries make the same products. Begin a discussion on dependence on other countries for goods. Tell students that most goods are transported from country to country by large ships. The goods are unloaded and then placed on trucks or trains and brought to stores near where the students live.

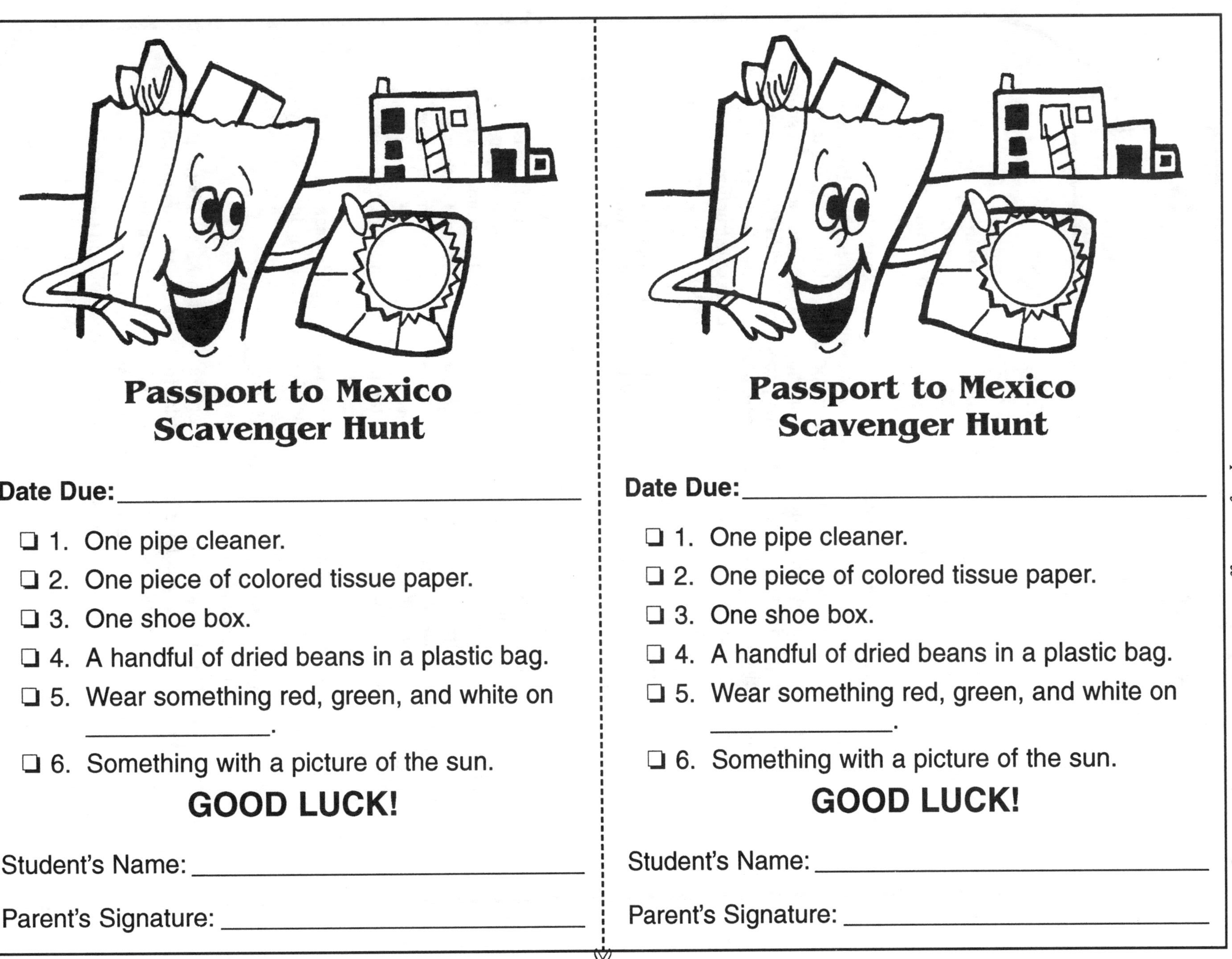

Passport to Mexico Scavenger Hunt

Date Due: ____________

- ☐ 1. One pipe cleaner.
- ☐ 2. One piece of colored tissue paper.
- ☐ 3. One shoe box.
- ☐ 4. A handful of dried beans in a plastic bag.
- ☐ 5. Wear something red, green, and white on ____________.
- ☐ 6. Something with a picture of the sun.

GOOD LUCK!

Student's Name: ____________

Parent's Signature: ____________

Passport to Mexico Scavenger Hunt

Date Due: ____________

- ☐ 1. One pipe cleaner.
- ☐ 2. One piece of colored tissue paper.
- ☐ 3. One shoe box.
- ☐ 4. A handful of dried beans in a plastic bag.
- ☐ 5. Wear something red, green, and white on ____________.
- ☐ 6. Something with a picture of the sun.

GOOD LUCK!

Student's Name: ____________

Parent's Signature: ____________

Passport to Mexico Scavenger Hunt (cont.)

Follow-up Activities

- Show your students on a world map, where Mexico is located. Ask them what other countries border Mexico and in what direction your country is from Mexico. Make a list on chart paper titled "What We Know About Mexico" and "What We Would Like to Know About Mexico." Brainstorm with your students to complete the chart.
- On the day that your students wear red, white, and green, show them the flag of Mexico. Remind them that a country's flag is a symbol representing how people feel about their country. Tell them red stands for union, white stands for religion, and green stands for independence. Point out the emblem of the eagle and snake. Explain that legend says one tribe of the first peoples of Mexico (the Aztecs) built their capital city where they saw an eagle perched on a cactus while devouring a snake. Have students make their own Mexican flags from construction paper.
- Tell students one of the first peoples of Mexico were called Aztecs. The Aztec Indians centered their life and religion around the sun. Allow students to share their sun objects. Point to Mexico City, the capital on the map. Explain to students the original capital city built in the 1300s, was called Tenochititlan and was in the same spot as today's capital. Write the word sun on the board. Ask students to list all the things the sun provides for us.
- Talk about the kinds of homes students live in. Ask them to describe their neighborhoods. Write the word pueblo on the board. Tell them a pueblo is a small town built around a church and central plaza. Explain to students that earlier pueblo houses were made from adobe, a mixture of clay, water, and a little bit of straw. Tell them that adobe bricks were made, they were laid in the sun to dry, and that is what houses were made of. Adobe houses are square in shape with wooden doors and small windows. Have students make adobe houses from their shoe boxes by painting the boxes with tan tempera paint. Create a pueblo with the adobe houses.
- Ask students to share any experience they have had eating Mexican food. Talk about the importance of rice and beans in the Mexican diet. Conduct a survey of the types of beans students brought in. Have students draw an outline of Mexico on a piece of construction paper, then glue their beans around the edges of the country. Add more details to the map as are age appropriate.
- Tell students that a traditional craft and decoration found in Mexico is the popular paper flower. Paper flowers have been popular for hundreds of years and still are today. The flowers vary in sizes and colors and are used in ceremonies and fiestas (parties). Collect tissue paper and have each student cut out three circles of different sizes from the tissue. Use scissors to poke two holes in the centers. Bend a pipe cleaner through the two holes so that the pipe cleaner is even at both ends. Twist the pipe cleaner, and this will create a flower. Decorate the room with the paper flowers.

Westward Ho! Scavenger Hunt

Date Due: ____________

- ❏ 1. If you could keep only one toy, what would it be? Bring in this toy.
- ❏ 2. A handful of grass in a plastic bag.
- ❏ 3. Three small rocks.
- ❏ 4. One matchbox.
- ❏ 5. One small square of aluminum foil about 2" x 2" (5 cm x 5 cm).
- ❏ 6. The capital letters W, E, S, T cut out of a magazine or newspaper.
- ❏ 7. Three words that rhyme with west cut out of a magazine or newspaper.

GOOD LUCK!

Student's Name: ____________

Parent's Signature: ____________

BEST
REST
TEST

Westward Ho! Scavenger Hunt

Date Due: ____________

- ❏ 1. If you could keep only one toy, what would it be? Bring in this toy.
- ❏ 2. A handful of grass in a plastic bag.
- ❏ 3. Three small rocks.
- ❏ 4. One matchbox.
- ❏ 5. One small square of aluminum foil about 2" x 2" (5 cm x 5 cm).
- ❏ 6. The capital letters W, E, S, T cut out of a magazine or newspaper.
- ❏ 7. Three words that rhyme with west cut out of a magazine or newspaper.

GOOD LUCK!

Student's Name: ____________

Parent's Signature: ____________

Westward Ho! Scavenger Hunt (cont.)

Follow-up Activities

- Show your students a map of the United States. Review directions with them, pointing to the two coasts and national borders. Ask them to point on the map, in the direction of west. Tell them about the early pioneers who left their homes in the east and traveled west across the country in covered wagons. Ask students what reasons people have for moving. Tell them that many of the pioneers left to start farms on inexpensive land, mine for valuable materials, or to create a better life for themselves.
- Show your students a picture of a covered wagon. Make a list of items that a family should take with them to start a new home. Talk about the challenge of fitting everything into a small space. Tell them that families often had to leave many valuables behind and make choices about what to take. Have students share their toy with the group. Ask them why they picked the toys. Encourage them to share what they think the pioneer children must have felt when they had to leave some of their toys behind.
- Refer to the map and point out the three most popular trails that pioneers traveled from Independence, Missouri—the Oregon Trail, the California Trail, and the Santa Fe Trail. Talk about the geographical features of each area and ask your students which trail they would have liked to have traveled. Discuss the kinds of hardships that the pioneers faced (e.g., bumpy ride, lack of shade and water in the Great Plains states, dangerous rivers and mountain ranges to cross, sometimes unfriendly Indians, getting caught in the snow, etc.). Tell students that they will be making "Heading West" maps. On construction paper have students trace the outline of the United States (younger students will need this done for them). Make marks for Independence, MO; Portland, OR; Sacramento, CA; and Santa Fe, NM. Using different colored pens, trace the three trails. Brush the Great Plains area with glue and press down the blades of grass. Glue (or tape) the rocks down to represent the Rocky Mountains. Make a miniature covered wagon from a match box and aluminum foil. Glue this along one of the trails. Write the word "Heading" on the map, then glue the four letters spelling "WEST" next to it. Map details will vary, depending upon age and ability.
- Write whole-group or individual poems about traveling west. Students must use each of their three west rhyming words in the poems at least once. Glue the cut-out words onto the actual places in the poems where those rhyming words fit.

Arbor Day Scavenger Hunt

Date Due: ____________________

- ❑ 1. One apple.
- ❑ 2. One leaf from a tree.
- ❑ 3. One small twig from a tree.
- ❑ 4. A magazine picture of a tree.
- ❑ 5. A food product with maple in it.
- ❑ 6. Your family tree written down on an index card, showing three generations.

GOOD LUCK!

Student's Name: ____________________

Parent's Signature: ____________________

Arbor Day Scavenger Hunt

Date Due: ____________________

- ❑ 1. One apple.
- ❑ 2. One leaf from a tree.
- ❑ 3. One small twig from a tree.
- ❑ 4. A magazine picture of a tree.
- ❑ 5. A food product with maple in it.
- ❑ 6. Your family tree written down on an index card, showing three generations.

GOOD LUCK!

Student's Name: ____________________

Parent's Signature: ____________________

Arbor Day Scavenger Hunt (cont.)

Follow-up Activities

- Tell students that Arbor Day is a national holiday for the United States and celebrated in some parts of Canada. Other countries also set aside days to celebrate and plant trees. Arbor Day began in the state of Nebraska. When people celebrate Arbor Day, they often think of Johnny Appleseed. John Chapman (a.k.a. Johnny Appleseed) traveled across the eastern part of the United States for 40 years, planting apple seeds and giving seeds and young trees to the settlers. Survey the different types of apples students brought to class. Make a floor bar graph showing the different types of apples. Have students estimate how many seeds are in their apples. With the help of another adult, cut each student's apple in half vertically. Students should count their seeds and compare the number to their original estimates. Ask students to save their seeds and eat their apples.
- Students will make pictures of trees, using the leaves, twigs, and seed. If necessary, break down the twigs so that they will fit onto pieces of white construction paper. Glue or tape the twigs to the papers. Students then draw the ground and sky. Glue the seeds from the apples at the base of the tree. Glue the single leaves to the tops of the trees and then draw some of their own. Some students may want to write poems about their trees or give their trees names. Display their pictures.
- Talk to your students about what kinds of things a tree provides to both humans and animals (e.g., shelter, food, enjoyment, etc.). Remind them of the importance of protecting this natural resource. Ask students to share their food products made with maple syrup. Tell them maple syrup comes from maple trees. If appropriate, allow students to sample some of the products. (Maple candy can be purchased at most health food stores if you wish to provide students with your own sample.)
- In small groups have students share their family tree information. As a large group, ask your students why they think a tree is used for family information. Students will take the pictures of the trees they collected and glue them to construction paper. Next they will glue their family tree cards to the center of the tree pictures. If the tree pictures are not large enough, use crayons or pens to enlarge them. Make a large empty tree for the bulletin board and display student family trees.
- With whatever financial resources you have available, purchase and plant a tree on your school grounds on Arbor Day. Spend ample time before the tree planting to research with your students what kind of tree would be most suitable for the climate, as well as most enjoyable for students in years to come. Work out a schedule for watering and fertilizing the tree.

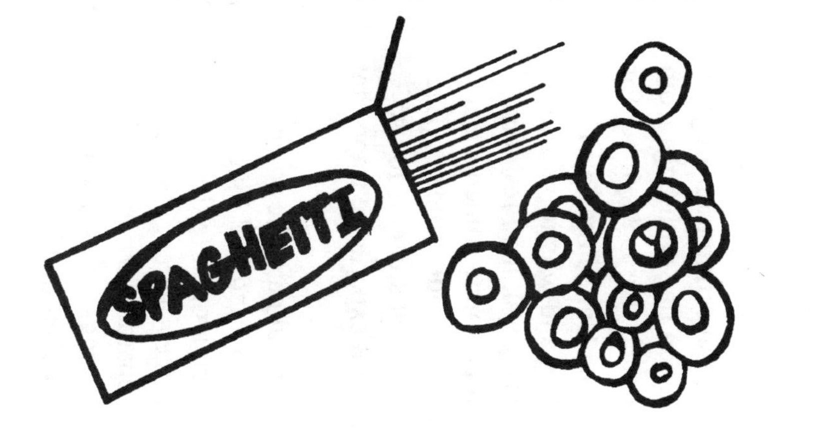

Flag Waving Scavenger Hunt

Date Due: ____________________

- ❑ 1. 50 Cheerios in a plastic bag.
- ❑ 2. 13 pieces of uncooked spaghetti.
- ❑ 3. Any picture of the United States flag, cut from a magazine, newspaper, photo, etc.
- ❑ 4. Any picture of a flag from another country.
- ❑ 5. An unused stamp with the United States flag on it.
- ❑ 6. Wear something red, white, and blue to school on.

GOOD LUCK!

Student's Name: ____________________

Parent's Signature: ____________________

Flag Waving Scavenger Hunt

Date Due: ____________________

- ❑ 1. 50 Cheerios in a plastic bag.
- ❑ 2. 13 pieces of uncooked spaghetti.
- ❑ 3. Any picture of the United States flag, cut from a magazine, newspaper, photo, etc.
- ❑ 4. Any picture of a flag from another country.
- ❑ 5. An unused stamp with the United States flag on it.
- ❑ 6. Wear something red, white, and blue to school on.

GOOD LUCK!

Student's Name: ____________________

Parent's Signature: ____________________

Flag Waving Scavenger Hunt (cont.)

Follow-up Activities

- Show the American flag to your students. Explain to them the flag is a symbol for a country. Tell them that the current American flag has 13 stripes and 50 stars which are symbolic of the original 13 colonies and the 50 states in the United States. Students will create their own American flags with Cheerios and spaghetti. Give each student a large piece of rectangular construction paper. Using rulers have them make squares in the upper left-hand corners. Students will then glue the Cheerios (stars) and spaghetti (stripes) in the appropriate places.
- Ask students to share their collected pictures of the flag. Compare and classify the samples by size, texture, and where found. Show students pictures of how the American flag has changed over time (or draw them on the board). The 1775 "Don't Tread On Me" flag, the 1777 "Stars and Stripes" flag, the 1795-1818 "Star Spangled Banner," and the current "Old Glory." Have students make a time line with these four flags. Brainstorm with them when and how the flag's design could change again.
- On a large piece of butcher paper attach or draw a world map, leaving a wide border around the map. After each student shares their flag pictures from other countries, have them glue their pictures on the large piece of butcher paper, outside of the world map. Then help students draw lines connecting their flags to the respective countries. Compare and contrast the American flag with flags from around the world. Ask students to share what they think each flag is a symbol for.
- Have students write individual letters to the President of the United States. Their letters should include what they have learned about the flag and why it is important to take pride in the country. Encourage students to ask the President questions, as well as offer comments and suggestions. Very young students can draw pictures of the flag and dictate their letters to an adult or older student. Each student will use the collected stamp for postage. You may want students to use their home addresses instead of the school's so that they will experience important letters being delivered to their homes.
- On the day the students wear red, white, and blue, play several patriotic songs such as "America," "Yankee Doodle Dandy," and "You're a Grand Old Flag." Host a parade inside the classroom and have students march around to the music. If they have made their own flags, they can wave them as they march. Take a group picture of your class and display it on the bulletin board. Take individual pictures of students, as well. Have students write poems, songs, or essays about the flag. Attach their photos to their writing samples for a class display.

National Symbols Scavenger Hunt

Date Due: ______________________

- ❑ 1. One quarter.
- ❑ 2. Any kind of ringing bell.
- ❑ 3. A small picture of the American flag.
- ❑ 4. Something red, white, and blue.
- ❑ 5. A flat sheet. (This will be returned in its original state.)
- ❑ 6. Two unsharpened pencils.

GOOD LUCK!

Student's Name: ______________________

Parent's Signature: ______________________

National Symbols Scavenger Hunt

Date Due: ______________________

❑ 1. One quarter.
❑ 2. Any kind of ringing bell.
❑ 3. A small picture of the American flag.
❑ 4. Something red, white, and blue.
❑ 5. A flat sheet. (This will be returned in its original state.)
❑ 6. Two unsharpened pencils.

GOOD LUCK!

Student's Name: ______________________

Parent's Signature: ______________________

National Symbols Scavenger Hunt (cont.)

Follow-up Activities

- Tell students a symbol is a picture or diagram that stands for something else. Different nations use different symbols to show their feelings about themselves and their land. Ask them to share any symbols they know. Tell them they will be learning about some of America's symbols and what they represent.
- Ask students to look at their quarters. Ask them to describe what they see. If they do not see the image on the tail side, tell them that it is an eagle. Tell students the bald eagle is America's national symbol. Ask them why they think the eagle was chosen. Brainstorm possible other animals that could be the national symbol. Tell them the eagle was chosen because it has great strength, flies high above the land, and has excellent vision. Share with students that over 200 years ago Benjamin Franklin wanted the turkey to be the national symbol because it was a wise and clever bird, in addition to being an important food source for America's early settlers. Show students a picture of a turkey and take a vote on which symbol they like best. Have students place a piece of writing paper over the eagle side of the quarter and rub a pencil over the surface to make a tracing of the eagle.
- Tell (or show) students about the Liberty Bell and how it is a symbol of liberty and freedom, that Americans believe in. The Liberty Bell was rung in 1776, when the United States declared its independence from England. Today it hangs in Philadelphia, Pennsylvania. Show students Philadelphia on a map. Ask them to show and ring their bells for the rest of your class. Play and/or sing patriotic songs and ring the bells during the songs.
- Tell students about the Declaration of Independence and its importance to the United States of America. Also tell them that this document has been saved and may be viewed by the public in Washington, DC. Explain that paper at that time in history was very different from the type of paper we use today. Explain to the students that scrolls were used. On rectangular strips of writing paper, have students glue their pictures of the American flag. Then tape the pencils to the ends of the papers and roll them up like scrolls.
- Have students share their red, white, and blue items. Point out these are the colors of the flag. Ask students why they think these colors were chosen. Tell students that Americans wear these colors when they celebrate Independence Day or other patriotic occasions.
- Show students a picture of the Statue of Liberty. Tell them this statue is a symbol for freedom and safety. She holds the torch that lights the way to freedom. Immigrants who traveled through New York Harbor would look for the Statue of Liberty to greet them. Have students drape the sheets around themselves in the toga fashion of the Statue of Liberty. In their left hands they can hold their scrolls and in their right hands pretend they are holding torches. Take pictures of these mini statues.

Thanksgiving Scavenger Hunt

Date Due: ____________________

- ❑ 1. A handful of unpopped corn in a plastic bag.
- ❑ 2. Two straws.
- ❑ 3. One toilet paper center roll.
- ❑ 4. A picture of a fish.
- ❑ 5. A picture of a turkey (e.g., cooked or live; from a newspaper, magazine, etc.).

GOOD LUCK!

Student's Name: ____________________

Parent's Signature: ____________________

Thanksgiving Scavenger Hunt

Date Due: ____________________

- ❑ 1. A handful of unpopped corn in a plastic bag.
- ❑ 2. Two straws.
- ❑ 3. One toilet paper center roll.
- ❑ 4. A picture of a fish.
- ❑ 5. A picture of a turkey (e.g., cooked or live; from a newspaper, magazine, etc.).

GOOD LUCK!

Student's Name: ____________________

Parent's Signature: ____________________

Thanksgiving Scavenger Hunt (cont.)

Follow-up Activities

- Ask students to share how they celebrate Thanksgiving. Ask them to tell how much they know about the first Thanksgiving and why they think the holiday happens in the fall. Show students Massachusetts and England on the world map. Tell them about the Pilgrims traveling from England to Massachusetts in order to start a new land and freely worship their religion. Ask students to brainstorm how they would have traveled to North America and in what direction.
- Tell students the name of the Pilgrims' ship was the *Mayflower.* Explain that there were many people traveling on the ship so it was very crowded, people became sick, and the journey took 65 days. Children on the ship did not have many places to play. Ask students to consider how these Pilgrim children would have amused themselves on the long journey. Have students make their own *Mayflower* ships. Cut an oval shape from one of the sides of the toilet paper roll. Use one large index card to cut out three different sized squares. Poke two holes in each of the squares and fit one square on one straw and the two squares on the other straw. Use a small piece of clay (or tape) to attach the straws to the base of the boat. Encourage students to use their ships to trace the journey on the class's large world map and ponder what the journey must have been like for the children their age.
- Tell students the Pilgrims arrived in Plymouth in December, and it was too late to plant crops. The women and children stayed on the boat through the winter, while the men lived on the land in caves and shelters made from mud and wood. Many people died. Explain how the native American tribe, Wampanoag, came to help the Pilgrims. They taught them how to successfully plant and where to hunt. One planting tip they gave the Pilgrims was to plant a dead fish in the soil along with the seeds. Ask students why they think this would help, then explain. Tell students one of the main crops grown was corn. Have students draw a picture showing an Indian helping a Pilgrim plant corn. Divide the paper in half horizontally and glue the fish picture and a few popcorn kernels in the soil.
- Tell students how in the following fall, the Pilgrim harvest was plentiful, and they celebrated their good fortune by having a feast with the Indians. Make a "Thanksgiving Foods" chart, divide it in half, and label the sides "Then" and "Now." Glue turkey pictures on both sides. Have students list their foods, then have them write down foods from the original feast (e.g., beans, berries, clams, corn, ducks, fish, geese, lobsters, peas, and squash). Establish the connection between living near the ocean and harvesting fish products.
- Make a time line of the Pilgrim events prior to the first Thanksgiving. Write the months on the line. Events to include: Arrival in Plymouth in December 1621, harsh winter months, Wampanoag helped with crops in spring, harvest in October, and feast in November.

The Four Seasons Scavenger Hunt

Date Due: ______________________

- ❑ 1. One old or blank calendar. (Banks often give away free calendars.)
- ❑ 2. One styrofoam sandwich container (or flat piece of styrofoam).
- ❑ 3. One large leaf from a tree.
- ❑ 4. One flower pressed between two pieces of tissue and paper towel.
- ❑ 5. A plastic bag with a small handful of sand.
- ❑ 6. Hats that could be used for each of the four seasons. (Hats will be returned.)

GOOD LUCK!

Student's Name: ______________________

Parent's Signature: ______________________

The Four Seasons Scavenger Hunt

Date Due: ______________________

- ❑ 1. One old or blank calendar. (Banks often give away free calendars.)
- ❑ 2. One styrofoam sandwich container (or flat piece of styrofoam).
- ❑ 3. One large leaf from a tree.
- ❑ 4. One flower pressed between two pieces of tissue and paper towel.
- ❑ 5. A plastic bag with a small handful of sand.
- ❑ 6. Hats that could be used for each of the four seasons. (Hats will be returned.)

GOOD LUCK!

Student's Name: ______________________

Parent's Signature: ______________________

The Four Seasons Scavenger Hunt (cont.)

Follow-up Activities

- Ask students what a season is and then name all four. If you have pictures showing the different seasons, share these with students. Ask students to tell what they know about each season. (If the seasons in your geographical area differ, talk about why this is, as well.) If any of your students' calendars have pictures illustrating the four seasons, have them share the pictures at this time.

- With students looking at the calendars they brought, go through the calendar, talking about each month and what holidays and seasons fall in each month. As you read through the calendar, have students use a marker or crayon and circle the holidays and their birthdays. When finished reviewing the calendar, ask students to cut out the names of each of the months.

- Have students make a seasons booklet, using the month names, styrofoam, leaf, flower, and bag of sand. Have students cut snowflakes from the styrofoam. Glue the snowflakes onto a piece of construction paper and write the word "winter." Next glue the month names, December, January, and February somewhere on the page. Use the leaf and September, October, and November words for "autumn." Use the pressed flower and March, April, and May for "spring." For "summer" spread glue on the bottom of the page and sprinkle the sand to make a beach scene, using the month words June, July, and August. Make a cover for the book and staple.

- Ask students to have all of their seasonal hats in their bags. Write the seasonal words on four index cards. Tell students when you hold up a season they must wear their hats for that season. Play this game several times by increasing the speed each time you hold up a word. Ask students to choose their favorite hats and have the rest of your class guess what season that hat should be worn. After the game, talk about why each hat is beneficial to wear during that season. Discuss why some hats would not be appropriate to wear during the wrong season.

Community Workers Scavenger Hunt

Date Due: ______________________

Collect an item representing each of the following jobs:

- ❑ 1. A doctor
- ❑ 2. A trash collector
- ❑ 3. A fire fighter
- ❑ 4. A police officer
- ❑ 5. A postal worker
- ❑ 6. A teacher
- ❑ 7. A grocery clerk

(Examples of items: stamp, tongue depressor, apple, story from newspaper about fire fighters rescuing people, grocery sack, etc.)

GOOD LUCK!

Student's Name: ______________________

Parent's Signature: ______________________

Community Workers Scavenger Hunt

Date Due: ______________________

Collect an item representing each of the following jobs:

- ❑ 1. A doctor
- ❑ 2. A trash collector
- ❑ 3. A fire fighter
- ❑ 4. A police officer
- ❑ 5. A postal worker
- ❑ 6. A teacher
- ❑ 7. A grocery clerk

(Examples of items: stamp, tongue depressor, apple, story from newspaper about fire fighters rescuing people, grocery sack, etc.)

GOOD LUCK!

Student's Name: ______________________

Parent's Signature: ______________________

Community Workers Scavenger Hunt (cont.)

Follow-up Activities

- Ask students to describe a community. Talk about the different people who live and work there and the interdependence upon one another. Explain that people usually work to earn money (income) to help them live, but many jobs also help other people in the community too.

- Write the names of the community workers on the board: doctor, trash collector, fire fighter, police officer, postal worker, teacher, and grocery clerk. Have students talk about what they know about these community jobs. Divide your class into seven groups and assign each group one of these jobs by drawing the job titles from a hat. Have each group role play a "Day in the Life of a ______" and ask the remaining groups to guess what job they are acting out.

- Play "Silent Symbols" with the items they brought. Write the seven jobs on the board and number them. For younger students you may want to draw pictures next to each word. Have students place their seven symbols in their bags and sit in a large circle. Go around the circle and have each student silently pull out a symbol and hold it up. As soon as the other students guess the job, they silently hold up their fingers in the number assigned to that job. When all students have made a guess the student showing the symbol silently displays the correct number.

- On seven large sheets of chart paper, write each of the job titles. As you talk about each job, have students share the symbols they brought representing that job. Brainstorm qualities and skills that people who perform these jobs should have. Write them down on the charts. If possible, glue or attach students' symbols on the charts.

- Survey students and determine which job of these seven they would most like to have. Create a line graph with the results. Ask students to draw conclusions about the information, such as "Most people would like to be teachers" or "Just a few people would like to be fire fighters."

- Have students write letters to community workers. The letters can be thank you's for all the hard work these people do to help their community. Encourage students to share what they have learned about these workers and ask any questions they may have. Younger students could simply draw pictures.

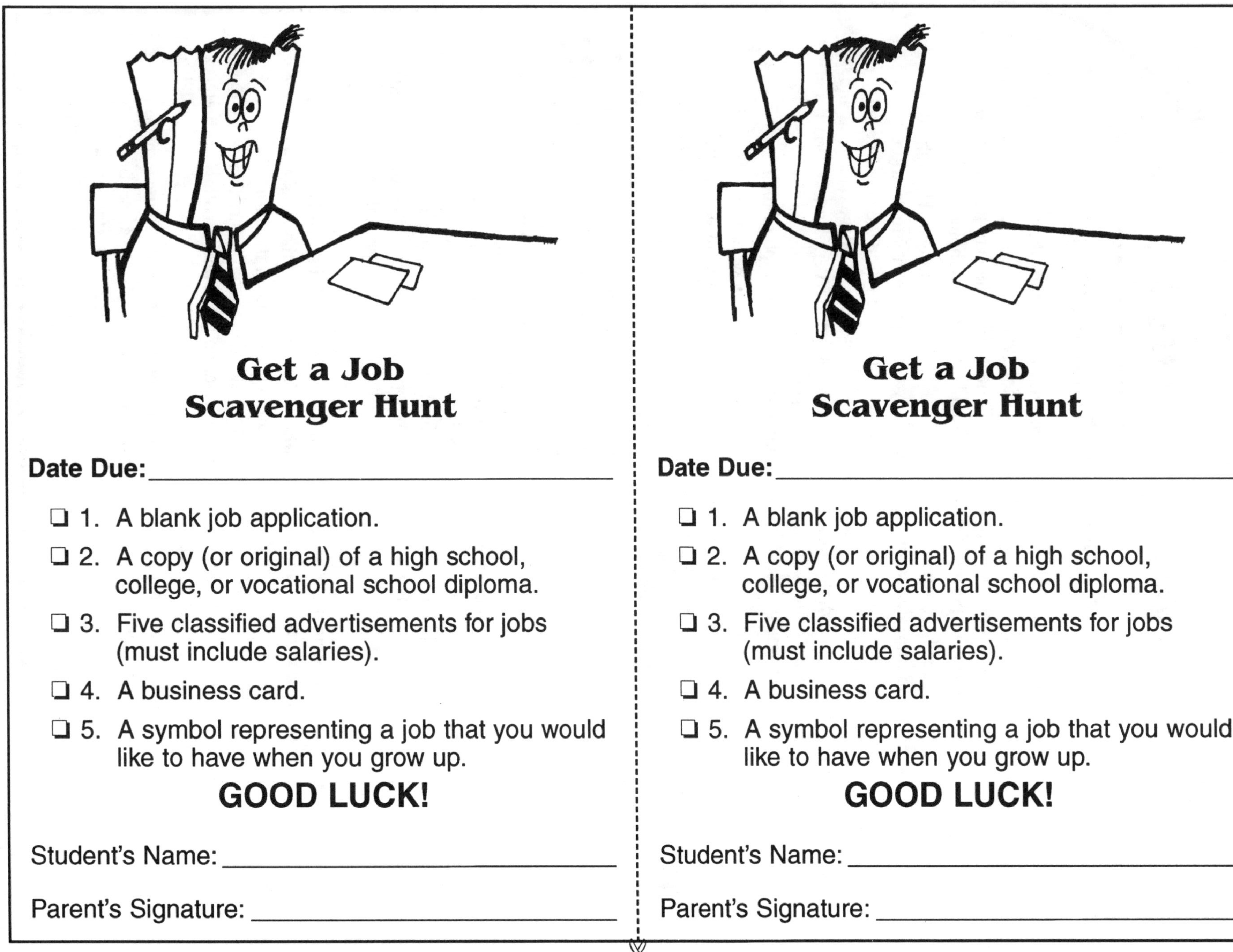

Get a Job Scavenger Hunt

Date Due: ______________________

- ❑ 1. A blank job application.
- ❑ 2. A copy (or original) of a high school, college, or vocational school diploma.
- ❑ 3. Five classified advertisements for jobs (must include salaries).
- ❑ 4. A business card.
- ❑ 5. A symbol representing a job that you would like to have when you grow up.

GOOD LUCK!

Student's Name: ______________________

Parent's Signature: ______________________

Get a Job Scavenger Hunt

Date Due: ______________________

- ❑ 1. A blank job application.
- ❑ 2. A copy (or original) of a high school, college, or vocational school diploma.
- ❑ 3. Five classified advertisements for jobs (must include salaries).
- ❑ 4. A business card.
- ❑ 5. A symbol representing a job that you would like to have when you grow up.

GOOD LUCK!

Student's Name: ______________________

Parent's Signature: ______________________

Get a Job Scavenger Hunt (cont.)

Follow-up Activities

- Ask students to share their symbols representing what jobs they would like to have when they grow up. Ask students to share why they chose these jobs and in what ways they could prepare for them. Collect all of the symbols and display them on a table (or poster, if possible) titled "Our Career Choices."
- In small groups have students share their classified job listings. They should share the job title, salary for the job, and any other pertinent information. Younger students will need an adult or older student to guide the small group. Each group should vote to decide what job sounds the best of the ones read and report back to the whole class. Write the job titles and salaries on the board and have each group share why they picked their job. Then conduct a survey to determine how many would choose which job. Make a graph of the results.
- Refer to the jobs listed in the above graph. Ask students what skills they think would be necessary to perform these jobs and how they would obtain these skills. Talk to students about the importance of finishing high school. Tell them about institutions for continued learning such as junior colleges, universities, and vocational and trade schools. Have students share the diplomas they collected. They should share whose it is, what kind of institution it came from, and any other details they choose. Talk about special certificates they can receive in school now and liken them to diplomas.
- In small groups have students share job applications. They should tell where they got the applications. Working in a group have them compare and contrast applications. With the large group make two lists on the board, "Alike" and "Different," writing the students' observations. Then write the word "Interview" on the board. Explain to them the interviewing process. Have students role play an interview by completing part of the job application (younger students may just write in their names) and in partners take turns being the applicant and interviewer.
- Have students write their names on the back of their business cards. In a large circle pass the cards around one at a time so that the rest of the class can observe them. Talk about what important information should be on the card. Give students small index cards and tell them to make their own business cards for the jobs that they currently do, either at school or at home. Make a collage of both real and pretend business cards.
- Brainstorm with students about how to go about getting a job. Review the job search and application process. Write down all of the tasks (e.g., school, diploma, training, look for a job, application, interview, etc.). Then ask students to number them in their proper order. Have students make time lines showing the order of how to get a job. Have them draw pictures for each task.

The Cost of Living Scavenger Hunt

Date Due: ____________________

- ❑ 1. A cancelled check (checking account number does not need to be seen).
- ❑ 2. An advertisement or flier for a service (e.g., lessons of some kind, pet grooming, baby-sitting, travel arrangement, car wash, etc.).
- ❑ 3. A receipt for a household bill such as garbage collection, utilities, phone service, cable, etc.
- ❑ 4. A bank savings deposit slip.
- ❑ 5. Five pennies.
- ❑ 6. Compare the price(s) of candy today to what it was when your parents were your age. Write the type of candy and prices for the past and present.

GOOD LUCK!

Student's Name: ____________________

Parent's Signature: ____________________

The Cost of Living Scavenger Hunt

Date Due: ____________________

- ❑ 1. A cancelled check (checking account number does not need to be seen).
- ❑ 2. An advertisement or flier for a service (e.g., lessons of some kind, pet grooming, baby-sitting, travel arrangement, car wash, etc.).
- ❑ 3. A receipt for a household bill such as garbage collection, utilities, phone service, cable, etc.
- ❑ 4. A bank savings deposit slip.
- ❑ 5. Five pennies.
- ❑ 6. Compare the price(s) of candy today to what it was when your parents were your age. Write the type of candy and prices for the past and present.

GOOD LUCK!

Student's Name: ____________________

Parent's Signature: ____________________

The Cost of Living Scavenger Hunt (cont.)

Follow-up Activities

- Ask your students if they have ever heard their parents talk about the cost of living. Ask them why they think living has costs. Ask them how people make money to pay for these costs. Tell them when people get jobs, the money they earn is called income. Explain that most of the income earned goes toward paying for the cost of living. Ask students to share what their parent(s) do to earn their income.
- Write the words *Goods and Services* on the board. Tell students that part of a person's income goes toward buying goods and services. Tell them that goods are things that people make for other people to use (e.g., cars, furniture, houses, and clothing). Write examples and have students add their ideas. Next tell them that a service is a useful act that people do for others in exchange for money. Have students share their advertisements for services. Write them on the chart and tally the repeated listings. Discuss with students what services they or their family have used. Remind them that the production of goods and services provides jobs for people, which in turn earns them an income.
- Write the Words *Income* and *Expenses* on a large chart paper. Explain that expenses are all the ways that income is spent. Have students share the bills they collected. Sort and group the bills according to type. Find out which are the most expensive and least expensive bills from the collection. Ask students what they think are the most important bills and why. Ask them what happens if they do not pay the bills. Talk about the importance of making and following a budget so people will not spend more than they earn.
- Ask students what goods their five pennies would buy them. Then ask them what they could buy if they and two other people combined their pennies. Establish the notion that five pennies may not seem like much, but over time the collection of pennies will lead to more money which will lead to greater options in spending. In small groups count all the pennies, then combine the totals to get a penny total for your class. Write the amount on the board and show how the pennies grew in value to more than a dollar. Ask students what they could do or buy with this combined amount of money. If no student suggests putting it into savings, do so. Ask students to brainstorm reasons why saving money is important. Have them share their savings slips. Create a large one for the class and write in the class amount on the slip.
- Have students share their information about the changing price of candy. Discuss and compare the results. Ask your students why they think the price has gone up. Write the word *inflation* on the board. Make predictions as to how much the price of candy will have risen by the time they grow up.

The Outdoor Worker Scavenger Hunt

Date Due: ____________________

- ❑ 1. A picture of a stop sign cut out from a magazine, a newspaper, or drawn.
- ❑ 2. A garbage sack.
- ❑ 3. One small piece of wood.
- ❑ 4. One leaf.
- ❑ 5. Two paper cups.

GOOD LUCK!

Student's Name: ____________________

Parent's Signature: ____________________

The Outdoor Worker Scavenger Hunt

Date Due: ____________________

- ❑ 1. A picture of a stop sign cut out from a magazine, a newspaper, or drawn.
- ❑ 2. A garbage sack.
- ❑ 3. One small piece of wood.
- ❑ 4. One leaf.
- ❑ 5. Two paper cups.

GOOD LUCK!

Student's Name: ____________________

Parent's Signature: ____________________

The Outdoor Worker Scavenger Hunt (cont.)

Follow-up Activities

- Have students share their stop sign pictures. Compare and contrast the different pictures. Ask students where they see stop signs and if they ever see people holding stop signs. Lead the conversation to the traffic police officer who directs traffic on busy corners, as well as diverts traffic for accidents or special events. Talk about what would happen if nobody was there to direct traffic, as well as the potential dangers of this job. Ask what other kinds of signs the traffic police officer uses. Create a collage of the stop signs; students may use them in their booklets or post around the school in necessary places.
- Discuss the job of a trash collector. Have students share their neighborhood situation with trash (e.g., does the company provide cans, what day is pick up, what is the truck like, where is the trash picked up, etc.). Ponder what the effects would be if there were no trash collectors in the world. Take a walk around your campus (and adjoining park, if applicable) and have students use their trash bags to collect trash. Dispose of the trash properly. Encourage students to personally thank their neighborhood sanitation engineer, if possible.
- Ask students to share their pieces of wood. Ask them what kinds of things could be made of wood. Mention the building of homes, office buildings, and other structures. Discuss the job of construction worker. Encourage students to tell of any construction sites they have seen. Talk about the kinds of tools and clothing a construction worker wears. Either divide students into groups or as a whole group, create a structure made with the wood pieces collected.
- Write the job title *park ranger* on the board. Talk about the responsibilities of this job and how they vary, depending upon which national park the ranger works for. Tell how the park ranger helps to protect the land. Lead a discussion about conservation and things students can do to help. On a large piece of construction paper make a list of these ideas, then create a decorative border with the leaves.
- Have students make a telephone system with the two paper cups. Give them each a piece of string, poke holes through the bottoms of the cups, thread the string through and tie knots on both ends. Allow students time to experiment and play with their phones. Write the job title *telephone repair person* on the board. Talk about whether students' telephone lines are above or under ground. Explain the dangers of climbing the telephone pole in order to repair a line. Ask students to ponder the effects of downed telephone lines.
- After students have completed their "Outdoor Worker Booklets," take a poll and determine what each student's favorite outside job would be. Make a class graph of the results. Encourage students to write letters of thanks to any one of these outdoor workers.

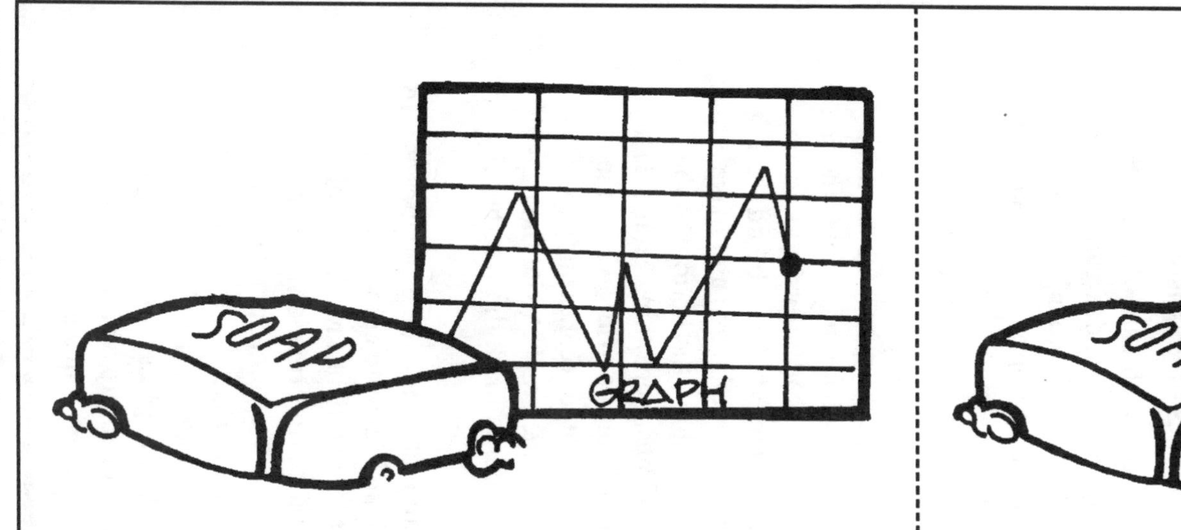

Graphs Galore Scavenger Hunt

Date Due: ______________________

- ❑ 1. One paper plate.
- ❑ 2. One bar of soap.
- ❑ 3. One washcloth. (With a pen, write your initials on the tag.)
- ❑ 4. A graph (e.g., line, bar, or pie) clipped from a newspaper, magazine, or brochure.

GOOD LUCK!

Student's Name: ______________________

Parent's Signature: ______________________

Graphs Galore Scavenger Hunt

Date Due: ______________________

- ❑ 1. One paper plate.
- ❑ 2. One bar of soap.
- ❑ 3. One washcloth. (With a pen, write your initials on the tag.)
- ❑ 4. A graph (e.g., line, bar, or pie) clipped from a newspaper, magazine, or brochure.

GOOD LUCK!

Student's Name: ______________________

Parent's Signature: ______________________

Graphs Galore Scavenger Hunt (cont.)

Follow-up Activities

- Write the word graph on the board. Ask your students if they have ever heard that word and what they know about graphs. Tell them a graph is a way to show a lot of information in an orderly manner. Tell them there are different kinds of graphs; some have pictures and some have lines. Have them share their graph clippings. Pass them around so students can see different types of graphs.
- Write the words *pie graph, line graph*, and *bar graph* on the board. Draw a sketch of each kind of graph. Tell students that different graphs can be used to show the same information. Have students tape their graph cutouts under the right heading. Draw conclusions about how many types of graphs were collected.
- **Bar Graph:** Make a large, real bar graph on the floor with bars of soap. Have students share what brand names of soap they brought. On index cards, write the various names and place the cards on the floor next to each other horizontally. Have students then place their bars of soap above the appropriate index card and begin making columns. When finished, point out the individual bars of soap have turned into long bars of soap. Have students copy the graph information on graph paper for reinforcement.
- **Line Graph:** (Data for this graph will be done two weeks prior. Observe the weather for 14 consecutive days and make notes as to what kinds of weather are experienced.) Tell students that a line graph is used to chart information over time. Make a large, real, line graph on the floor (or large bulletin board), using the wash cloths. Lay the cloths down (or pin them on the board) and make a quilt so that a large rectangle is created with four squares along the bottom of the graph. You may need to bring a few more wash cloths, depending on the data you choose. Tell students that the squares (wash cloths) form a grid. Along the left side of the graph use index cards to write types of weather (e.g., sunny, partly cloudy, rainy, snow, windy, etc.). For the bottom of the graph, write the days of the week on index cards. Use an eraser or other item to mark the weather for each day, then connect the markers with yarn.
- **Pie Graph:** Students will use the paper plates to make individual pie graphs. To gather data for this graph conduct a poll of students' favorite colors. Write four color choices on the board and tally the numbers for student favorites. Tell students they will make pie graphs showing this data (information). Using your own paper plate, explain how to divide the plate into fractional parts that represent the number of students for each color. Work in approximations for the purposes of concept development. Students follow your lead and cut pie pieces from their plates to represent each color. Have them color the pie pieces and then put the pie back together again. (Depending upon age level and ability, you many want to introduce the concept of fractions and/or percentages with this activity.)

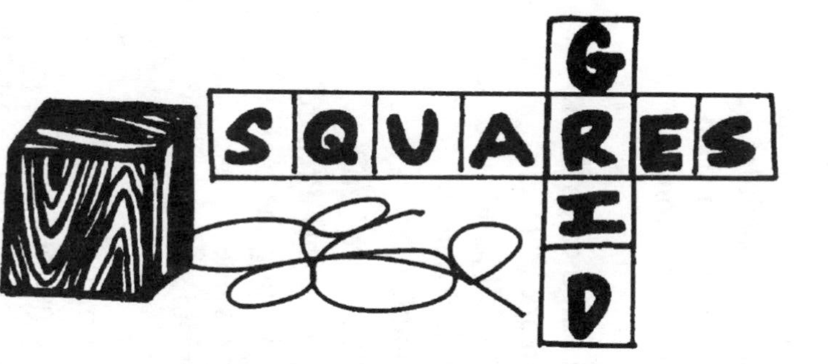

The Great Grid Scavenger Hunt

Date Due: ____________________

- ❑ 1. Two index cards with the name of a city in your state written on each card (other than the city you live in).
- ❑ 2. Something made with, or that uses, squares.
- ❑ 3. Find something in your home or neighborhood which shows two lines crossing and draw a quick picture of it.
- ❑ 4. One square piece of cardboard 10" x 10" (25 cm x 25 cm).
- ❑ 5. A piece of string (yarn, twine, or thin rope will also do) approximately 20' (6 m) long.

GOOD LUCK!

Student's Name: ____________________

Parent's Signature: ____________________

The Great Grid Scavenger Hunt

Date Due: ____________________

- ❑ 1. Two index cards with the name of a city in your state written on each card (other than the city you live in).
- ❑ 2. Something made with, or that uses, squares.
- ❑ 3. Find something in your home or neighborhood which shows two lines crossing and draw a quick picture of it.
- ❑ 4. One square piece of cardboard 10" x 10" (25 cm x 25 cm).
- ❑ 5. A piece of string (yarn, twine, or thin rope will also do) approximately 20' (6 m) long.

GOOD LUCK!

Student's Name: ____________________

Parent's Signature: ____________________

The Great Grid Scavenger Hunt (cont.)

Follow-up Activities

- Have students share their square items. Draw a square, circle, triangle, and rectangle on the board and ask students to point out the differences and similarities among the shapes. Explain that a square is an equal length on all four sides. Tell students there is a special type of map that uses squares to help people locate places. This kind of map is called a grid.
- Allow students time to share their pictures of things with intersecting lines. Have them explain how the lines intersect. Refer to a grid and point out that it is a map with many intersecting lines.
- Show your students an actual grid map or draw a make-shift one on the board. Point out that across the top there are numbers and down the sides there are letters. Explain how to locate a point inside the grid, using the letters and numbers.
- On a large piece of butcher paper, draw the outline of your state (use an overhead projector to enlarge and project the image onto the paper, if you wish to trace). Use a state map for your reference, if needed, as you have students glue their index cards of city names to the map in their appropriate locations. Create a grid for the map by stapling strands of yarn. Write (or attach index cards) the letters and numbers across the top, bottom, and sides. When the map is finished, let students take turns locating cities by calling the grid letter and number for each. Point out that this is a quicker method of finding a location than by random scanning. Students can add more cities to the map as they wish.
- Play bingo to reinforce the letter and number grid skill. Make bingo cards from the cardboard squares your students brought in. Use rulers to mark 2" (5 cm) squares and write the numbers and letters on the outside squares. Students choose city names from the large class map to fill in their bingo squares. Younger students may fill in the squares with circles, triangles, and rectangles.
- Turn your classroom (multipurpose room or grass area) into a "kid-size" grid. Have students tape down in criss-crossing lines the strings they brought. Prepare number and letter cards with plain writing paper and place them along the outside edges of the grid. Call out letter-number combinations and have students take turns finding a location. Once the square is found, students remain standing in that square until all students are placed on the grid.
- Show your students a globe and point out the equator and prime meridian as the main grid dividers for the earth. Have students take turns with a partner, naming places and determining whether it is a place north or south of the equator and east or west of the prime meridian.

The World at Large Scavenger Hunt

Date Due: ______________________

- ❑ 1. One cup (250 g) of white flour in a plastic bag.
- ❑ 2. One piece of string approximately 24" (60 cm) long.
- ❑ 3. The lid to a medium size cardboard box (or one of the sides of the box).
- ❑ 4. Seven toothpicks.
- ❑ 5. Seven white, stick gum wrappers.
- ❑ 6. The name of a country on a continent other than where you live, cut from a magazine or newspaper.

GOOD LUCK!

Student's Name: ______________________

Parent's Signature: ______________________

The World at Large Scavenger Hunt

Date Due: ______________________

- ❑ 1. One cup (250 g) of white flour in a plastic bag.
- ❑ 2. One piece of string approximately 24" (60 cm) long.
- ❑ 3. The lid to a medium size cardboard box (or one of the sides of the box).
- ❑ 4. Seven toothpicks.
- ❑ 5. Seven white, stick gum wrappers.
- ❑ 6. The name of a country on a continent other than where you live, cut from a magazine or newspaper.

GOOD LUCK!

Student's Name: ______________________

Parent's Signature: ______________________

The World at Large Scavenger Hunt (cont.)

Follow-up Activities

- Show students a world map. Tell students that there are seven large areas of land in the world. Explain that these large areas are called "continents." Point to each continent one by one. Then tell students that there are four large bodies of waters called "oceans." Point to each ocean one by one. Point to the continent where you live. Locate your country. Emphasize the great distances between continents and talk about ways of traveling to each. Then ask students to locate the continents and oceans on the globe. Talk about the difference between a world map and a globe.

- In partners, have students look at maps of the world. Point out each continent and ask them to trace their fingers around the shapes. Talk about which is the biggest, smallest, connected to what ocean and other continent, etc. Have students place their fingers on a given continent, then tell them to locate another continent using a direction.

- Tell students that they will be making a map of the world using baker's dough. With the flour students collected, add salt and water into mixing bowls. Make enough so that each student will have a substantial ball of dough. Dough Recipe—2 cups (500 g) flour, 1 cup (250 g) salt, 1 cup (250 mL) water. Using pencils, have students draw the outlines of the continents on the cardboard pieces. Then they can form dough into the shapes on the cardboard. While the maps begin to dry, students will make flags for each continent, using the toothpicks and gum wrappers. Have either students or an older helper write in the names of the continents on the wrappers. Then wrap and tape one end of each wrapper around the toothpick. Stick the flags into their respective places on the map and let map continue to dry. When maps are dry, students can use tempera paint to color the oceans and land masses.

- Show your students a world map and globe again. Point to the equator. Tell students that the equator is the imaginary line which divides the earth in half. Point out some of the countries located around the equator and explain the tropical weather they experience. Have students attach their pieces of yarn across the middle of their maps to indicate the equator.

- Ask students to share the names of the countries they cut out of the newspaper. Explain the difference between a continent and a country. Then help students locate their countries on the map and identify the continents they are on.

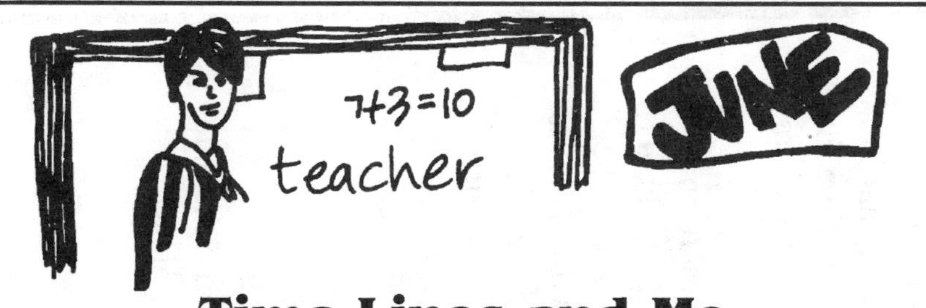

Time Lines and Me Scavenger Hunt

Date Due: ____________________

- ❑ 1. A cut-out word of one of the twelve months.
- ❑ 2. An item representing your first year of life.
- ❑ 3. An item representing your second year of life.
- ❑ 4. An item representing your third year of life.
- ❑ 5. An item representing your fourth year of life.
- ❑ 6. Something which represents you in the present.
- ❑ 7. Something which represents what you want to do or be in the future.
- ❑ 8. The date (month, day, and year) that your oldest living relative was born (written on a piece of paper or index card).

GOOD LUCK!

Student's Name: ____________________

Parent's Signature: ____________________

Time Lines and Me Scavenger Hunt

Date Due: ____________________

- ❑ 1. A cut-out word of one of the twelve months.
- ❑ 2. An item representing your first year of life.
- ❑ 3. An item representing your second year of life.
- ❑ 4. An item representing your third year of life.
- ❑ 5. An item representing your fourth year of life.
- ❑ 6. Something which represents you in the present.
- ❑ 7. Something which represents what you want to do or be in the future.
- ❑ 8. The date (month, day, and year) that your oldest living relative was born (written on a piece of paper or index card).

GOOD LUCK!

Student's Name: ____________________

Parent's Signature: ____________________

Time Lines and Me Scavenger Hunt (cont.)

Follow-up Activities

- Write the words time line on the board. Tell your students that a time line is a way to show events in order over the course of time. Draw on the board a horizontal line with 12 equally distributed vertical marks. Tell students that this will be a time line representing the year. Ask students who have the cut-out word "January" to take turns taping their words beneath the first mark. Continue this process for the remaining months. Point out to students the importance of order. Next add important dates (e.g., birthdays, holidays, vacations, etc.) along the time line to reinforce the idea of events occurring over time.
- Choose a literature story that your class has read. Make a list of all the main events that happened in that story. Draw a line on the board with several marks. Ask students to plug in the events of the story in the order they occurred. Tell them they have just made a time line for that particular story.
- Have students share their future items. Encourage them to give details about why these items were chosen and, in particular, at what point in the future they are referring. Tell your class as they share, you will be making a Future Time Line of their information. Draw a line on the board (or paper) and begin the time line with today's date. As students share their items and future time, make a mark for each student, listing the student's name and the item brought. When the time line is finished, review the results with the students. Talk about the advantages of this kind of tool to help keep track of information in an orderly manner.
- Tell students that they will be making time lines of their lives. Give each student a thin strip of butcher paper approximately four feet (120 cm) long. Help them to make the necessary marking points on the time lines. Each time line should begin with the year of that student's birth. Student names should also be written on the time lines. Have students write the subsequent years/dates on the other marks. Have students place their personal items on the time lines along the appropriate marks. The marks for their future items will differ. Lay the time lines along counters, tables and/or on the floor. Students will tour the class and view each of the time lines.
- Make a time line called "Our Relatives" with the information that the students collected. Determine the oldest living relative, and that will serve as the beginning of the time line. When marking the remaining relatives, write the date, as well as titles such as "Timmy's great-grandma" or "Brenda's great-uncle."

Scavenger Hunt

Date Due: ______________

❑ 1. ______________________________

❑ 2. ______________________________

❑ 3. ______________________________

❑ 4. ______________________________

❑ 5. ______________________________

❑ 6. ______________________________

GOOD LUCK!

Student's Name: ______________________

Parent's Signature: ____________________

Scavenger Hunt

Date Due: ______________

❑ 1. ______________________________

❑ 2. ______________________________

❑ 3. ______________________________

❑ 4. ______________________________

❑ 5. ______________________________

❑ 6. ______________________________

GOOD LUCK!

Student's Name: ______________________

Parent's Signature: ____________________

Scavenger Hunt

Follow-up Activities

Awards

I FOUND ALL OF THE ITEMS IN THE
CONGRATULATIONS!
SOCIAL STUDIES
SCAVENGER HUNT
Name:
Date:

Awards

I HUNTED DOWN A HARD-TO-FIND ITEM IN THE

TREASURE MAP.

Start

SOCIAL STUDIES
SCAVENGER HUNT

Name: ______________________________

Date: ______________________________

